FOR OFFICIAL USE ONLY.

40 W.O. 6969.

Notes for Instructors

ON

The Use of the Rifle.

(Cancels "A Sequence of Musketry Training.")

ISSUED BY THE GENERAL STAFF.

October, 1918.

The Naval & Military Press Ltd
© 2008

In reprinting in facsimile from the original, any imperfections are inevitably reproduced and the quality may fall short of modern type and cartographic standards.

PREFACE.

Definition of an Instructor.

An Instructor is an Officer or N.C.O. capable of—

       (a) Training the recruit in the use of the rifle.

       (b) Refreshing the trained man.

       (c) Training an officer or N.C.O. to be a fire unit leader.

These notes have been divided into three parts to enable the instructor to understand clearly the matter to be dealt with and the methods applicable in each case.

    PART I.—The training of the Recruit.

    PART II.—The refreshing of trained and semi-trained men, *i.e.*, returned Expeditionary Force men at home, or men " out of the Line " abroad.

    PART III.—Deals with the subjects in which a fire unit leader must be proficient.

The notes consist chiefly of headings setting forth the sequence in which each subject should be imparted, and should be read in conjunction with M.R. Infantry Training and Bayonet Training.

They will enable the instructor to refresh his memory by reference to the text books, and they form summaries for lectures.

PART I.

THE TRAINING OF THE RECRUIT.

	PAGE
Notes for Instructors	4
Care of Arms and Ammunition.—To ensure that the rifle is kept in such a condition that it will always be capable of accurate and rapid shooting.	5
Theory	6
Visual Training.—To see the enemy; recognise aiming points; confidence when alone; ability to report what has been seen; ability to understand instructions.	7
Judging Distance.—To know whether enemy is within individual range; to know what range to use.	8
Aiming Instruction.—Ability to aim correctly at any object, however difficult, whether seen or described.	10
Firing Instruction.—Ability to use the rifle correctly in all positions in the open and behind cover.	12
Muscle Exercises.—Strength to fire continuously	12
Fire Discipline Training.—The use of all the above combined, and elementary training in working as one of a unit.	15
Miniature Range.—Shooting under easiest possible conditions ...	17
30 Yards' Range.—Shooting under easiest possible conditions with service ammunition.	19
Range Practices.—Knowledge of rifle and confidence in it at known individual ranges; practice in its use under varying conditions.	19
Individual Field Practices.—Application of fire at unknown range up to 600 yards under approximately service conditions. *See* Appendix.	22
Section, Platoon, and Company Training.—The combination of fire and movement: fire discipline and tactics.	23
Collective Field Practices.—The practical application of all previous training with ball ammunition.	23
APPENDIX...	24

NOTES FOR INSTRUCTORS.

Moral.—" The object to be aimed at in the training of the infantry soldier is to make him mentally and physically a better man than his adversary on the field of battle."

Moral is born of confidence, and confidence can only be acquired by men who know that they possess skill in the use of their weapons. From the day the recruit first handles his rifle the instructor must impress upon him that the rifle is his chief means of winning a battle. Whether he uses the bullet or the bayonet he must be made to realise that it is for one purpose, and for one purpose only, namely, to kill an opponent. The realisation of this principle produces the true fighting spirit, and it is essential that this spirit should permeate the whole of the training of the soldier.

The fighting spirit, founded on confidence in his weapons and fortified with discipline, should imbue the soldier with the desire to come to grips with his opponent. Skill with the rifle will enable him to bring the issue to a successful conclusion.

There are two methods of killing with the rifle: firstly, with the bullet, outside the rifle's length; and, secondly, with the bayonet, within it. Both will be taught by the same instructor.

Sound methods of training should enable the appropriate use of each to become second nature to the soldier.

General Methods.—Teach, Practise, Test.—Lessons in any one subject should never exceed ¾ hour, and may frequently be shorter.

The foundations of good marksmanship are laid during the recruit's elementary training. Instruction must therefore be thorough, progressive and systematic; faults must not be passed over, but must be immediately corrected. An instructor who fails to detect mistakes and omits to correct them in a simple and reasonable manner is useless.

As soon as individual perfection has been attained it must be combined with smartness and rapidity.

The knowledge possessed by the instructor is necessarily wider than that required by the recruit, only essentials should be imparted.

Paragraphs marked * are mainly for the information of instructors. In respect of other portions of Part I not so marked instructors must use their discretion.

Necessary explanations should be as brief as possible, they must invariably be illustrated if the matter permits. During periods of rest men should have explained to them the practical application of what they are being taught and should be frequently catechised.

Tests of elementary training may be carried out from time to time during instruction to ascertain a man's progress. The competitive spirit should be fostered in the section, and men encouraged to practice manipulation of the rifle, &c., off parade.

Discipline.—Although individual instruction is an essential feature of elementary training, and methods should be as little mechanical as possible, no relaxation of discipline must be allowed.

Any tendency to slackness or inattention must be at once checked and may be corrected by the introduction of words of command and such simple collective drill as the squad is capable of performing.

The instructor must keep a close watch upon himself; he is the pattern for his squad; he must make his **personality felt**, he must be clear, concise and forceful; he must infuse life and energy into his instruction; he must possess that confidence in himself which can only be acquired by a thorough knowledge of his subject, and he must remember that good instruction requires at all times the full mental and physical energy of both instructor and pupil.

CARE OF ARMS AND AMMUNITION.

As soon as the recruit receives his rifle he should be given one hour's instruction:—
  20 minutes: Care of arms (cleaning).
  20 minutes: Trigger-pressing.
  20 minutes: Accuracy of aim.

Instructors will impress upon the recruit that the rifle is the soldier's first weapon for offence and defence; the most important part of his equipment; its powers both as regards accuracy and rapidity in skilled hands; useless unless in proper working order; its life and accuracy depend upon the care bestowed upon it; ordinary precautions to take against damage in barracks or on service, mud, sand, rifle covers, the breech stick, browning; stripping forbidden.

Causes of wear.—(a) Friction of bullet; (b) heat from explosion of charge; (c) pull-through gauze. [M.R., 85, 86.]*

Cleaning Materials.

Pull-through.—How to pack in butt trap; the three loops; danger of using much worn cord. [M.R., 87.]
Free from grit. [M.R., 89.]
The gauze.—Method of attaching; well oiled; fit tight. [M.R., 89.]
When used. [M.R., 90, 99.]
Flannelette.—Regulation only; dry, 4 in. × 2 in.; oiled, use smaller piece. [M.R., 88.]
Oil.—Work well into flannelette. [M.R., 91.]
Result of excessive quantity. [M.R., 88.]
Names of parts to be taught as required during cleaning, &c.
Cleaning of rifle.—Remove bolt and magazine; pull through from breech to muzzle; one steady pull; avoid cord wear. [M.R., 88.]
Daily cleaning. [M.R., 96.]
Before firing. [M.R., 97.]
After firing ball and blank. [M.R., 98, 99, 100, 101.]
Use boiling water when possible after firing.
Clean action (bolt and body) and outside of rifle with an oily rag.
Check number of bolt with that of body.
Clean inside of magazine with a dry rag.
Clean bayonet. [M.R., 115.]
Gas attack.—Precautions and cleaning. [M.R., 117B.]

Ammunition.

Keep dry and clean; avoid extremes of temperature; never oil the case. [M.R., 116.] Precautions during and after gas attack. [M.R., 117B.]

MECHANISM.

(Weights and measurements not required.)
Removing and replacing bolt. [M.R., 94, 95.]
Removing and replacing magazine platform. [M.R., 47.]
Safety catch; bolt lever in lowest position. [M.R., 44.]
Half cock and how to recock. [M.R., 42.]
Bolt-head screwed fully home. [M.R., 46.]
*Breech mechanism. [M.R., 35-44.]
*Examination of Arms.—[M.R., 118, 102.] Particularly barrel (dry clean), sights, safety catch, bolt and magazine.
Jams and remedies. (See Firing Instruction.)

THEORY.

NOTES FOR LECTURE.

References:—*Musketry Regulations, Sections 17 to 30.*

*I.—*Definitions* (146, 147).

II.—*Before the bullet leaves the rifle.*
*(1) RIFLING.
Definition.—See M.R., Section 19.
*(2) *Force of explosion.*—Causes bullet to move from "lead" to muzzle, leaving latter at 2,440 f.p.s., when Mark VII ammunition is used.
*(3) *Jump.*—Caused by shock of discharge, and to a certain extent by friction between bullet and rifling.
Jump of two kinds:—
(a) Vertical.
(b) Lateral.
As regards (a), whether upward or downward, depends on position of muzzle at moment bullet reaches it. Serious changes caused by altering muzzle velocity.
Vertical jump allowed for by different heights of foresight.
As regards (b), caused by lack of symmetry and differences in strength of different parts of rifle. Allowed for by lateral movement of foresight.
(4) *Fixing bayonet.*—Weight of bayonet damps vibrations, hence jump is altered. [M.R., 159, 160, 160A.] Fit of bayonet also affects amount.
(5) *Resting rifle.*—Does not affect jump if properly rested, therefore shooting unaffected.
(6) *Heated barrel.*—Causes bore to expand, thereby fit of bullet in bore impaired. Bullets fall short after prolonged rapid fire.
(7) *Oily barrel.*—Not of much importance. Causes loss of friction, therefore alters jump. [M.R., 163.]

III.—*After the bullet leaves the rifle.*
*(1) *Resistance of air.*—Checks flight of bullet, e.g., bullet (Mark VII) leaves muzzle travelling at rate of about 800 yards per second. Resistance of air allows it to travel only 600 yards in 1st second, 400 yards in 2nd second, 300 yards in 3rd second.
*(2) *Gravity.*—Draws bullet downwards with ever-increasing velocity. Thus path or trajectory of bullet is curved instead of straight.

(3) *Elevation and sighting.*—Necessary to allow for fall of bullet due to gravity, by directing line of departure as much above target as bullet would fall below it. Sights provided to enable this to be done, and at same time keep target in view. (Demonstration of trajectory with tracer ammunition and trajectory poles.)
*(4) *Drift.*—See M.R., para. 156.
(5) *Dangerous space.*—See M.R., Section 26. Show comparative vulnerability of standing, kneeling and prone figures with tapes.
(6) *Angles of descent.*—Necessary to know, since they affect the dangerous space. Individual fire to great extent limited by size of dangerous space. (Demonstrate only for recruit.)

IV.—*General.*
Ricochets.—See M.R., para. 168.
Wind and light.—See M.R., Section 30.

V.—*Sounds caused by rifle fire.* (Best illustrated by a demonstration.)
Two sounds are made when a rifle is fired—the noises of the explosion and the noises of the bullet passing through the air. When the bullet is going faster than sound, the latter noises reach the ear of an observer who is in front of the rifle as a single sound or crack which is much louder than the noise of the explosion. When bullets are fired across the front of an observer this noise appears to come from a point well down the course of a bullet, and is therefore no guide as to the position of the firer.

VISUAL TRAINING.

NOTES FOR LECTURE.

NECESSITY FOR INVISIBILITY AND HOW OBTAINED.
  Necessity on account of:—Accuracy of modern weapons.
  Obtained by:—(i) Close study and use of ground. [I.T., 108.]
              (ii) Suitable formations. [I.T., 90 and 118.]
              (iii) Night training. [I.T., 113.]
              (iv) Neutral tinted uniforms.
              (v) Smokeless powder.

TRAINED EYESIGHT NECESSARY OWING TO INVISIBILITY OF ENEMY.
  When—(i) on battlefield; (ii) working alone. [M.R., 306; I.T., 110.]

DIFFICULTIES TO BE OVERCOME.
    (i) Differences in sight: town and country.
    (ii) Brain power not developed.
    (iii) Lack of words—MILITARY VOCABULARY. [M.R., 310.]

STANDARD TO AIM AT.
  "That of a stalker."
  1. Ability to distinguish enemy from surroundings.
  2.   ,,   ,, aim accurately at service marks.
  3.   ,,   ,, report on what seen.
  4.   ,,   ,, recognise objects described.
  5. Establishment of feeling of self-reliance.
  6. Study and use of ground.

USE OF FIELD GLASSES.
  Usually to confirm what has been seen with the naked eye, but may be used to search for special targets. [M.R., 309.]

A SYSTEM OF INSTRUCTION.

For the private soldier:
Instruction must begin early and be progressive. [M.R., 307.]

BARRACKS.

Lectures. Men taught to recognise their immediate surroundings.
Training on landscape or Solano targets. [M.R., 280.]
Training on landscape targets or Solano targets. [M.R., 280.]

OPEN COUNTRY.

Object.—To teach men to locate low service targets up to 800 yards. [M.R., 306.]

(a) *Silhouette targets*, of different sizes, shapes, and colours, arranged against various backgrounds. Limits of areas in which targets are, clearly marked. Targets counted. Their characteristics and positions described. Reasons for difference in their visibility brought out. [M.R., 308.]

(b) *Fatiguemen.*—Instead of targets. Movement quickly detected. Blank used to train ear to locate sound. [M.R., 308.]

(c) *Practice.*—Two squads assume service positions and try to locate each other. [M.R., 309.]

EXAMINATION OF GROUND.

Object.—To enable men to make clear reports, to understand instructions, and to recognise features of military importance. [M.R., 309; I.T., 110.]

(a) *Definite line* in landscape. Described in detail.

(b) *Areas of ground.*—Clearly defined boundaries. Description of general shape. Natural and artificial features. Trees and fences. Fields, &c. Features of military importance brought to notice by questions. Military vocabulary largely increased.

As progress made.—Squad examines ground and gives description from behind cover. Limited time given for examination by squad; then squad turned about to give description. Large areas divided into sections: foreground, middle distance, and background.

(c) *Road work.*—Cultivate an eye for country by making men observe what they pass on the march. Question them after a given interval.

RECOGNITION.

Object.—To train the firer to recognise targets described. *Recognition* means a soldier's understanding of the exact point at which his commander wishes him to aim. [M.R., 306, 308.]

Practice in recognition.—Officer or N.C.O. describes aiming point. Men lay rifles on point recognised (aiming at ground).

On landscape targets squad turns about, and each man separately shows *exact* point of aim with a stick.

Test of elementary training.—Each man should recognise four points. [M.R., 299 (ii).]

JUDGING DISTANCE BY EYE.

Recruits, up to 600 yards. [M.R., 314.]
Trained soldiers, up to 800 yards, up to which distance they should not make a mean error of more than 100 yards. [M.R., 304, 323.]

Officers, non-commissioned officers, and selected men up to 1,400 yards. Beyond that distance, judging is very inaccurate and instruments are probably available. [M.R., 303, 324.]

The limit of individual fire (600 yards) must be recognised by all. [M.R., 314.]

The MEAN of the estimates of several individuals is generally more reliable than the estimate of one individual.

A SEQUENCE OF INSTRUCTION.

Unit of measure.—Some familiar distance is used as a unit; generally necessary for men to be taught one; 100 yards is a convenient unit; the class place themselves independently at what they think is 100 yards from an object; the distance between the farthest and nearest is paced; 100 yards is measured accurately from the object; the class is shown the correct unit. This method can only be used when the whole of the ground to be measured is visible: the unit is applied to ground between the class and flags; fatiguemen are not used, otherwise this method may be confused with others; examples are shown to which this method cannot be, or can only be partly, applied. [M.R., 312.]

Appearance.—The appearance of men in different positions, and of objects of known size, is studied and noted, at various distances and under all conditions of light, background, atmosphere, &c. [M.R., 312, 314.]

The followng points should be noted:—

  (1) The apparent height of the object.

The foresight, or other guide, may be used for comparing the apparent height of objects at different distances. [M.R., 318.]

  (2) Appearance of the heads and shoulders of men.
  (3) Distinctness of outline.
  (4) Distintness of the face, hands, rifle, and head-dress.
  (5) Movements when loading and firing.

Appearance varies with eyesight of individuals; a classification range is suitable for the early lessons ; the system is applied to men, then to objects of known size.

Opportunities for revising the impressions of the appearance of men at various distances, should sometimes be given. [M.R., 319.]

Objects are over-estimated when they are difficult to see or when the eye is attracted by other objects. Objects are under-estimated when they are clearly distinguishable. [M.R., 315.]

Comparison with known ranges and similar methods [M.R., 317, 318]:—

  (1) This includes trying to halve the distance, and judging the half-distance first.
  (2) Judging to some object of known size, and then getting the distance by comparison.
  (3) Judging with the assistance of range cards.

Bracketing.—Decide on the longest distance the object can be; decide on the shortest distance the object can be; take the mean. [M.R., 317.]

Practice.—Constant practice is necessary under all circumstances, both in peace and war, as serious errors must be expected under strange conditions. [M.R., 305.]

Methods should be combined till distances can be approximately judged by the general impression conveyed to the eye. [M.R., 313.]

Time limits should be gradually introduced after the first lessons. [M.R., 318.]

To prevent guessing, reasons should be given by everyone for their estimates. [M.R., 316.]

Sights should be adjusted to the estimates given.

Lying in the open or suitable positions behind cover, should be used normally when judging distance. [M.R., 325 (ii).]

By constant practice, mean errors should be reduced to 10 per cent., but an average error of 15 per cent. must be expected; records of results should be kept. [M.R., 305.]

AIMING INSTRUCTION.

NOTES FOR INSTRUCTORS.

Sights.—The sights of all rifles must be in perfect order (M.R., 200). They will always be adjusted to the actual distance during this instruction.

Length of Lesson.—Should not exceed 30 min. [I.T., 4 (6), 10 (3).] Each Lesson will be repeated as necessary until the recruit is proficient, before proceeding to a more advanced one.

System of Instruction.—To illustrate principles or check faults a free use will be made of large diagrams on paper, blackboard or ground; by practical illustration with the rifle, and by the use of most suitable appliances; *e.g.*, accuracy of aim—paper in front of muzzle, the Le Gret aim teacher only in very exceptional cases; rapidity of aim—aiming disc; aiming off for movement—the aim corrector

Individual instruction is necessary. [I.T., 10 (1).]

Progressive sequence of instruction is essential. [I.T., 10 (4).]

Instruction to be combined with Visual Training, Judging Distance and Fire Orders in the later stages.

Preliminary Arrangements.—A brief lecture of explanation should precede the carrying out of the various lessons, where required. A pre-arranged programme is necessary to enable N.C.O's to carry out the instruction.

SEQUENCE OF INSTRUCTION.

1. Absolute Accuracy.

Sights.—Reasons for. [M.R., 152.] Illustrate with bolt removed.
Graduations. [M.R., 30.] Method of adjusting. [M.R., 31.]
Men practice.
Instructor checks. [M.R., 202.]

Correct Aim.—Laid from an aiming rest and tripod at the following targets:—

(a) Bullseye up to 100×.

(b) Figure targets 200×—400×   ⎫ Increase the distances of
(c) Silhouette targets up to 600× ⎬ targets up to these limits
  ⎭ as progress is made.

Explain method of using sights (3 rules); diagrams. Focus target, not sights.
Men practice.
Instructor checks.

Common faults, explained as they occur, may be demonstrated by paper: Le Gret only necessary with very backward men. The correct point of aim at a man (or silhouette) at $100^\times$ or under is the waist.

Reasons for aiming at centre of lowest part of mark.—Whole mark is kept in view; better chance of hitting a vanishing target; better chance of hitting if distance over-estimated; counteracts tendency to shoot high; (assists close grouping in collective fire).

Reasons for full sight.—Less tendency to vary amount of foresight; facilitates rapid aim.

II. Aiming off for Wind:—Necessity for explained.

Auxiliary aiming marks will be used throughout to show correct aim.

(a) Small bullseye at $10^\times$: no measurements: method of keeping elevation: diagrams.

(b) Figure targets $200^\times$–$400^\times$: judging feet.

(c) Silhouettes $200 \times$–$600 \times$: target breadths.

Descriptions of various winds, size of targets, and a working knowledge of wind table.

WIND TABLE.

	300	500	
Mild	1 foot	2 feet	Halve allowances for oblique winds.
Fresh	2 feet	4 ,,	
Strong	3 ,,	6 ,,	

In aiming off all distances are taken from centre of lowest part of mark; a target's breadth will be measured from the edge of the target.

III.

For alteration of sights or point of aim in individual fire the recruit requires instruction in:—

(a) *Elevation Table.*

Range.	Elevation.	Vertical Rise Mark VII.
200	300	6 inches.
300	400	12 ,,
400	500	20 ,,
500	600	30 ,,
600	700	42 ,,

The use of the table should be taught with full size targets at actual distances with marking disc to show the supposed strike of bullets. (Lessons II and III (a) should be combined in a collective exercise.)

(b) *Aiming Up and Down.*

Object.—To avoid necessity of making petty alterations of sights. [M.R., 217, 221.]

Limited to three feet above or below regulation point of aim [M.R., 226.]

Figure targets first then silhouette.

IV. Accuracy and Rapidity of Aim (Essential for rapid fire and snap shooting).—Not to be taught until men have learnt prone position.

The object is to quicken the aim while retaining absolute accuracy and proper trigger release.

Time may be saved (1) In coming to the aiming position.
(2) In not dwelling on the aim.

Men practice.—Instructor checks with aiming disc. [M.R., 299, viii.] Snap shooting at vanishing targets at actual distances. Early lessons at short distances with long exposure, targets in the same place each time; later lessons up to $300^\times$; shorter exposures, targets appear in different places.

V. Aiming off for movement.—[M.R. 222.]

Mechanical movement of rifle shown from aiming rest with aim corrector. Practise swing and trigger release.

TABLE OF ALLOWANCES.

Man walking	... ...	1 ft.
Man doubling	... ...	2 ft.
Horseman trotting	... ...	3 ft.
Horseman galloping	... ...	4 ft.

per 100 yards.

For oblique movement halve allowance.
Limit: Single man, 300 yds.; horseman, 500 yds.
Practice at actual distances up to $300^\times$.
Instructor checks.
(Lessons III. (b), IV., and V. should be combined in a collective exercise.)

VI. Aiming at ground, etc.
At natural objects, features of ground up to all distances.
Point will be described by the Instructor.
(Recognition will be taught previous to this exercise.)

VII. Aiming off for wind. Collective practice over $600^\times$.
Necessary for officers and N.C.O.s to know wind table. [M.R., 638a.]

Point of aim indicated:
(1) By use of auxiliary aiming point.
(2) With reference to breadth of target.
(3) ,, ,, ,, intervals in a formation.
(4) (If above impossible) in yards and feet.

FIRING INSTRUCTION AND MUSCLE EXERCISES.

The essential points of the firing positions are to be insisted upon from the beginning as the foundation of fire discipline. [M.R., 227.] The instructor's attention is called to the main points (a) to (g) in the first stage of fire discipline training.

The press-off of all rifles should always be in **perfect order.** [M.R., 108.]

Rifles must fit the firers. [M.R., 119.]

Individual instruction necessary; small squads; normal positions suit nearly all men. [M.R., 228, 229; I.T. 4 (4).]

A section may be gathered round the instructor for the purpose of explanation; for practising the firing positions a bow shaped formation or a straight line may be adopted; in both cases great care must be taken that all men are facing so that their lines of fire are parallel, sufficient targets must be provided to enable this to be carried out. [M.R., 228.]

Method.—Illustration; explanation; imitation; examination. [I.T., 10 (2).]

Firing rest may be used if necessary. [M.R., 231.]

Dummy cartridges must always be used, but must be carefully inspected. [M.R., 262; I.T., 4 (8).]

Firing instruction should proceed simultaneously with aiming instruction. [M.R., 199.]

Progressive sequence of instruction essential. Sequence must fit in with stages reached in other branches of instruction, *e.g.*, men not allowed to snap till they have learnt correct aim, trigger pressing, correct firing position. [I.T., 10 (4).]

Targets used should be similar to those used in Aiming Instruction according to progress.

TRIGGER PRESSING. [M.R., 232–237.]

Most important.

Forefinger capable of independent movement; grip of three fingers and thumb; use of and position of forefinger on trigger; direction of pressure; double pressure required.

First pressure taken as butt is brought into the shoulder [M.R., 250]; second when aim is correct; breathing restrained during second pressure.

Recruit sitting; right elbow below the heel of the butt; rifle rested on sandbags; butt not to be in shoulder.

Instructor's hand over recruit's; recruit's hand over instructor's; concentration of mind necessary; practice.

POSITIONS IN THE OPEN.

* The " points to note," given on plates XIX.–XXX. M.R. are only for the instructor's information to guide him in checking and correcting faults.

STANDING.—Targets pointed out; complete firing position shown.
When used. [M.R., 240–241.]

Note.—The recruit will follow and imitate the instructor's movements step by step during the early instruction in each of the lessons (i), (ii) and (iii).

(i) *Loading position.* [M.R., 242.]
   Method of reaching position, first imitated, then practised; faults corrected. [I.T., 10 (5).]
* (Sequence of checking; if feet wrong, everything else is, so start at feet.)
   Reasons for half-turn, etc., should only be given during periods of rest.

(ii) Method of Loading. [M.R., 242.]
   Method of Adjusting Sights. [M.R., 244.]
   Method of Unloading. [M.R., 243.]

} Imitated; practised; faults corrected.
On unloading sights will be brought to normal.

(iii) *Firing position.* [M.R., 249.]

Method of reaching position; imitated; practised; faults corrected. [M.R., 250.]

Completed firing position, trigger pressed, point of aim declared. [M.R., 198, 235, 252.]

Reasons given during periods of rest.

Note.—To avoid tiring the men the instructor, for purposes of brief explanation or demonstration, may give the order " Rest." when safety catches will be applied and an easy position assumed; the men will return to the loading position on the order " Position."

For tests of Elementary Training, *see* Appendix.

MUSCLE EXERCISES (*See* Appendix).

Muscle exercises should proceed simultaneously with aiming and firing instruction. [M.R., 199.]

If performing more than one exercise the command "Unload" will only be given after the last.

Object; conspicuous target; rifle always approximately aligned and first pressure taken; practice daily by recruits, constantly by trained men; all positions. [M.R., 266.]

POSITIONS IN THE OPEN—*continued.*

The following are taught and tested on the same principles as the standing position. Detail of motions already taught will not be given:—

LYING. [M.R., 253–255.]

KNEELING. [M.R., 256 (ii).]

SITTING. On ground on which this position would be used [M.R., 256 (1).]

*Remedies for Common Faults.
1. Eye too close to cocking piece:—
    (a) Raise butt in shoulder.
    (b) Draw head further back.
    (c) Assume less oblique position.
    (d) Issue a rifle with longer butt.
2. Lack of grip:—
    Muscle exercise No. 2.
3. Varying position of butt in shoulder:—
    Muscle exercise No. 1.

POSITIONS BEHIND COVER.

When engaged with the enemy every man will be in observation; if not engaged a look-out or sentry will keep watch.

Eyes must be kept on target between shots [I.T., 108 (5)], but it is permissible to glance down to insert a fresh charger.

Artificial and natural cover.—[M.R., 257–259; I.T., 108.]

All positions will be taught: squad views from the front; correct uses of cover explained; each kind of cover used discussed—walls; loopholes; trenches; shell holes, etc.

Folds in the ground, etc., and cover from view demonstrated; practice in using suitable positions on broken ground. Isolated cover (round).

Points to bring out:—
1. Modification of position to suit cover, *without sacrificing fire effect*.
2. Rifle properly rested.
3. No undue movement or over exposure.

Rapid Loading.

Practised in all positions. [M.R., 261.] *See* Appendix: Rapid fire training.

Test of elementary training.—[M.R., 299 (ix.).]

Jams are due to:
(1) Faulty manipulation:—Always work the bolt rapidly and draw it back to its full extent; force it home cleanly in one motion.
(2) Dirt in magazine: *See* instructions for cleaning. [M.R., 103.]
With bolt drawn back give bottom of magazine a sharp blow with palm of the hand, or press the points of cartridges sharply down with the thumb and withdraw it quickly.
(3) Dirty ammunition:—Keep dry and clean.
(4) Some mechanical defect:—Fixed lips of magazine bent or magazine casing dented.—Take to armourer.

Rapid Firing.

(Not to be taught till a man can fire deliberately in all positions.)

Rapidity in loading and aim combined; accuracy necessary; rifle loaded in shoulder. [M.R., 260.] *See* Appendix: Rapid fire training.

Test of elementary training.—[M.R., 299 (x).]

Automatic Alignment

is the involuntary action of the muscles in carrying out correctly what they have constantly practised; consists of bringing the rifle to the shoulder and aligning the sights before pressing the trigger; constant practice and correction of faults in peace essential for this to be done correctly in war. [M.R., 197.] Muscle exercise No. 1 will be found useful in this respect.

FIRE DISCIPLINE TRAINING.

References—I.T., Sec. 117; M.R., Sec. 55.

A form of training which ensures that men obey orders rapidly and accurately, and, when left to themselves, use their rifles to the best tactical advantage.

After sufficient progress in aiming and firing instruction, practice will be given in moving in extended order. [M.R., 267; I.T., 90.]

Preliminary collective exercises consist of simple practices to teach accurate and quick obedience to fire orders, and to practise quick concentration of fire on various targets. Divided into two stages. [M.R., 276.]

The first stage of this training is simply drill, no tactical considerations. Second stage, lessons more advanced. [I.T., 90 (5).]

Normal firing position is lying; this will always be used unless other orders are given. The instructor will always make certain that the aiming mark he describes is visible to every member of his section. [M.R., 285; I.T., 92 (4).]

Standing, kneeling and sitting positions will only be practised under conditions when they would be used, or, in wet weather the position used may be standing or kneeling, when this will be explained beforehand, and such position will be used without further orders. [M.R., 286.]

Rapid fire should never be ordered or allowed unless the target justifies its use.

An assumed position of the enemy, always to be pointed out, to which men turn when halted. The position of the instructor must be that assumed by the fire unit commander until he has completed his fire orders; he will then move about and check faults. [I.T., 92 (3) (6).]

1st Stage.

Easy aiming marks used, and ranges given must be approximately correct. Section halted at ease, extended in line to one or two paces. The instructor gives orders for loading. He then gives the range, and the men adjust their sights. The fire orders are then completed, and the men act on them. They will continue to fire until the order to " Cease fire," " Unload " or " Advance " is given, or until the named number of rounds have been fired. [M.R., 285.]

The passing of orders along the line should also be practised. The main points for the instructor to note are:—

(a) Position assumed by the firer, dexterity in manipulation of bolt, loading, safety catch, and pouch buttoned.
(b) Correct adjustment of sights.
(c) Recognition of the target.
(d) Difference between " Rapid " and " Deliberate " fire.
(e) Difference between " Cease fire " and " Unload."
(f) Re-charging of magazine.
(g) Alertness of the men in attending to fresh orders.
(h) Passing of orders. [M.R., 288; I.T., 96 (2).]

• Every irregularity must be checked.

When the section is proficient at the halt, movement will be introduced.

Rifle loaded before the exercise begins; the men are responsible for keeping their magazines charged. The section advances in an extended line.

On the command or signal " Halt," the section assumes the lying position (unless otherwise ordered). Fire orders are given (particular attention being paid to correct pauses so that each part of the order may be acted on before the next is begun).

The instructor will walk round his section, paying attention to the points previously mentioned.

Passing of orders will also be practised. [I.T., 96 (2).]

2nd Stage.

Movement; use of ground and cover; initiative and judgment. Section advances in an extended line.

A fatigueman appears (for about a minute). Instructor orders, " At the fatigueman—Fire." Section halts, each man assumes the position he thinks suitable, adjusts his sight, and fires. [M.R., 290, 291.]

The instructor will first take up his correct position as commander, and then act as in " 1st Stage." [I.T., 92 (8).] As proficiency increases, more difficult targets used, *e.g.*, men or carts passing on road, &c. Change of targets, aiming off, &c. [M.R., 291.]

Anticipatory orders may sometimes be given in this stage. [M.R., 292.]

Some of the duties of the soldier in fire discipline:—
  (1) Recharge his magazine on every possible opportunity.
  (2) Make proper use of the safety catch.
  (3) In advance, to get up and down quickly. [I.T., 92 (5).]
  (4) When advancing select his next halting place, and move straight to it.
  (5) Make best use of cover.
  (6) Never press the trigger unless his sights are aligned on the mark. [I.T., 116 (12).]
  (7) Observe the enemy.

In Collective Fire.

  (8) Adjust sight for range ordered.
  (9) Recognise aiming point described.
  (10) Count the number of rounds fired if necessary. [M.R., 273.]
  (11) Limit his rate of fire to that ordered.
  (12) Pass orders. [M.R., 288.]

In Individual Fire. [I.T., 116 (2), 123 (12-14).]

  (13) Carry on the fight.
  (14) Select targets.
  (15) Judge distance.
  (16) Adjust sight.
  (17) Alter point of aim from observation.
  (18) Use rate of fire necessary.
  (19) When possible join nearest commander.
  (20) If wounded place ammunition where it will be found, and never discard arms and equipment.

MINIATURE RANGE.

For outdoor ranges, *see* M.R., Part II. (91-109).

Range Discipline.—Rifles should always be laid down with the breeches open when anyone is in front of the firing point. [M.R., II., 90; M.R., I., 367.] When rifles are being loaded, unloaded, or inspected, they should be directed towards the target.

Equipment—

Cover of all kinds can be made with sandbags; trenches should be made where possible.

Rifles should be service rifles bored for miniature ammunition, so that firers may become accustomed to the weight, length, balance. bolt action and sighting of the rifle he would use in war, otherwise miniature shooting cannot be a satisfactory preparation for service shooting. [M.R , II., 85.]

Rifles must be cleaned after every 20 rounds. [M.R., II., 88; I., 366, 105.]

SERVICE RIFLE, solid bore ·22; latest pattern has floating striker. [M.R., II., 86; I., 49.] Correct sighting for direct hits, 300. [M.R., I., 360; 49 (12).] PARKER RIFLING.

Aux. Aperture Sight.—L.C. War M., 18981, Aug., 1917.

Ammunition.—Only miniature ammunition may be used on a miniature range.

Target apparatus should be suitable for:—
  (a) Range practices.
  (b) Individual field practices.
  (c) Collective field practices.

(A) *Hythe Pattern*, useful for outdoor ranges. Sawdust or turf banks, former very good for observation practices.

(B) *Solano Pattern*, 10 feet, Mark I.

Accessories drawn to scale for use at 25 yards, yet the difficulties of service shooting can only be partly reproduced, *e.g.*, difficulty of estimating range; effect of wind; effect of atmosphere on bullet; effect of atmosphere on eyesight; shock of discharge.

Training.—A certain standard of training necessary before shooting begins. (Good prone position—accurate aiming and trigger pressing.)

Range practices.—With or without a rest or cover, various positions.

Grouping.—Rings 1, 2, and 3 inches. Recruits must reach a 3-inch standard.

Application.—First at bullseye targets, then at figure targets and silhouettes. Wind gauge may be used to represent necessity for wind. [M.R., 359, 356.]

Snapshooting.—First at figure targets, later at silhouette targets. [M.R., 363.]

Crossing Targets useful for practising movement of the rifle. [M.R., II., 197; M.R., I., 363.]

Rapid Fire.—Magazine ·22 Rifle, Mark I., and adapter experimental.

Individual Field Practices.—Most individual field practices can be fired using Solano figures representing men up to 600, and then target apparatus with scenic accessories.

Collective Field Practices.—The necessity for collective fire can be shown and many useful field practices carried out on the Solano target, or on landscape targets.

Landscape Targets.—The frame for landscape targets is 10 ft. long and 5 ft. high. Landscape pictures in sheets, 5 ft. by 2 ft., are pasted on to the lower portion, leaving 3 ft. of blank sky-screen above to receive the shots. [M.R., II., 156.]

Many of the landscapes are more than 2 ft. high, and must be cut down, as this necessitates very high backsight elevation, and affects the safety of the range. Frequent change of landscape targets is desirable, as the features become well known. When firing at landscape targets the rifles should be given extra elevation so that the bullets will strike the blank sky-screen, even if aim is taken at an object at the bottom of the landscape. Average elevation required is 1,400×. So that all the rifles should hit at the same height above the aiming point they should be harmonised. A board should be hung in every miniature range, showing the elevation required for shooting at landscape targets. [M.R., II., 157.]

For suggested miniature range course, *see* Appendix.

30-YARDS RANGE.

Very useful at all times, especially when classification ranges are distant for training recruits, and for indifferent shots throughout the year, with service ammunition. [M.R., 369; II., 46.]

Desirable that each unit should have one. [M.R., II., 48.]

Lateral protection greater than normal danger area of a classification range. [M.R., II., 54.] Amendment, *see* Gen. No. 11/932 (F.W. 1) 2/7/18.

Load with rifles pointing towards targets, otherwise a shot clearing the top of stop butt would go at least 2,500 yards. [M.R., 369.]

Suitable for all practices which can be fired on miniature ranges. [M.R., II.; 47.]

Advantages over miniature ranges:—

Man uses his own service rifle of which he knows the pull-off [M.R., 369.]

Learns to shoot with it under easy conditions. [M.R., 369.]

Becomes accustomed to the shock of discharge, and any tendency to flinch is eliminated. [M.R., 369; II., 46.]

Becomes accustomed to noise of discharge which is greater than on an open range. [M.R., II., 51.]

Rapid fire with service cartridges can be used. Practice in loading with service ammunition. [M.R., II., 46.]

Practice with long-range sights is possible. [M.R., 370.]

RANGE PRACTICES.

STAGES IN MUSKETRY TRAINING OF SOLDIERS.
 (1) Elementary training. [M.R., 343, 350.]
 (2) Training on miniature and thirty-yards ranges. [M.R., 354, 369.]
 (3) RANGE PRACTICES. [M.R., 5.]
 (4) Individual field practices.
 (5) Collective field practices. [M.R., 516.]

Range practices are an advanced stage of elementary training, and must be regarded as such. Object, to ensure that a certain standard has been reached by the soldier before he goes on to more practical shooting, and to give him confidence in his rifle and in his ability to kill. They are only fired up to 600 yards, the limit of individual fire. [M.R., 415.]

The individual musketry training of the soldier is not complete till he has become a good service shot. Range practices are simple as compared with service shooting; in some respects directly opposed to service methods. [M.R., 591.]

STANDARD.

Constant practice in handling the rifle is necessary to enable a man to become a reliable shot. Standard in elementary work ensured by tests of elementary training. Range practices only a waste of ammunition if this standard is not attained. [M.R., 351, 238, 296.]

When Fired.

Under as favourable weather conditions as the exigencies of training will permit.

Range Discipline.

Strict range discipline is necessary to prevent accidents, and facilitate instruction. Correct marking in the butts is essential. For officers' and N.C.O.s' duties at firing points and in Butts, see M.R., Section 91. Men not actually firing or waiting their turn to fire should be receiving instruction in the bayonet in addition to the subjects mentioned in M.R. 467: blob sticks gallows and where possible assault courses should be provided on rifle ranges.

Firing Positions and Use of Cover.

Regulation positions are obligatory in all range practices except those fired from behind cover, when the positions must be adapted to the cover, consistent with getting good fire effect. Cover must not be specially prepared as a rest. [M.R., 391, 462, 457, 449, 256 (2), 446, 455.]

Basis of Practices.

A course of range practices is based on a system of progressive instruction, and every practice is framed to illustrate some tactical use of fire, or some essential point of elementary training.

Grouping.

Grouping means firing a series of shots, usually 5, at a distinct aiming mark without any alteration of sighting or point of aim. Not fired at distances over 100 yards. The diagram made by the shots is called a group. [M.R., 378, 443, 381.]

Grouping brings out the necessity for:—
Absolute accuracy and consistency of aim, correct holding and trigger pressing, and control of the nerves; it enables the instructor to ascertain the firer's faults, and the firer learns which errors his rifle possesses.

Sights will be at 200× and windgauge central.

Men should see their groups measured and discussed.

The method by which the cause of a bad group is discovered is called the " analysis of faults." [M.R., 384.]

Analysis of Faults. [M.R., 379.]

Rifle is tested by an expert shot to show the soldier that the rifle is not to blame, or to discover if the rifle is inaccurate.

Aim tested from an aiming rest.

Trigger pressing, tested with aim corrector.

Sight tested, near, by reading; distant, by counting distant objects. [M.R., 382.]

Nerves the probable cause, if the above are correct. [M.R., 383.]

When a man has made a bad group, his faults should be analysed at once before leaving the range. A note should be made on the register of remedies to be used. [M.R., 381, 384.]

If Rifle is at Fault.

A soldier should not be expected to make considerable allowances to counteract the error of his rifle. [**M.R., 123.**]

21

He must fire with his own rifle. [M.R., 458.]
Throw of the rifle should be corrected by the armourer. [M.R., 130, 131.]

APPLICATION.

Application practices follow grouping; these teach the firer to adjust his sight and point of aim, so as to apply his shots to a mark. Application brings out the necessity for consideration of the wind and elevation, confidence in his rifle and powers of shooting, and ability to aim for the next shot according to the point of aim at the moment of firing and the result of the last shot. [M.R., 386.]

A man must be able to group before he can hope to apply with confidence. [M.R., 386, 444.]

As correction in sighting is seldom possible in individual firing in war, it is most important to estimate the elevation and point of aim for the first shot. [M.R., 418, 419.]

Time limit for each shot in slow practices 20 seconds. [M.R., 445.]

Men must note and memorise the sighting elevations required by their rifles at each distance.

SNAPSHOOTING.

Snapshooting means firing an effective shot in the shortest possible time. These practices bring out the necessity for watching the front, quickness of aim, observation of the strike of the bullet, change of point of aim from observations, and immediate reloading. [M.R., 395, 447, 449.]

RAPID FIRE.

Rapid fire means firing as many rounds as possible with accuracy in a given time. Rapid fire brings out the need for clean and quick loading, and handling of arms, quickness of aim and working the bolt with the rifle in the shoulder. These practices give men an opportunity of finding their best rate. [M.R., 394, 447, 450, 449, 397; I.T., 116 (12).]

When rapid and slow practices are fired at the same distance in classification, each man may fire the rapid immediately after the deliberate practice. [M.R., 438.]

Range practices begin with qualifying practices: if the standards are not reached preliminary training has failed in its object. [M.R., 373.]

GENERAL MUSKETRY COURSE.

Divided into four parts. Part I. Fired at short ranges to give confidence. (For qualifying standards and repetition, see Add. IV, M.R.)

Part II. (Is instructional.) The conditions are more difficult. The coloured figure target prevents men dwelling on their aim, taking a fine sight, or focussing the foresight instead of the target at the moment of firing. [M.R., 393.]

Rapid fire and snapshooting are introduced.

Part III. Is the test on which a man is classified. Instruction will still be given.

Part IV. Individual and Collective Field Practices. *See* Field Practices. For instructions, *see* Add. IV, M.R. Examples of suitable practices are given in the Appendix.

Allotment of Ammunition.
See Add. IV, M.R.

FIRING-POINT INSTRUCTION.

1. An instructor can only watch one man at a time, so men fire singly. [M.R., 461.]
2. The man must be watched, not the target, or faults cannot be discovered. [M.R., 376, 392, 390, 391.]
3. No hurry should be allowed; it is better to discuss the reasons for failure of a few shots properly than to hurry over many. [M.R., 442.]
4. A true declaration of the actual point of aim at the moment the rifle was fired must be made before the shot is signalled, so that true deductions can be made. [M.R., 390.]
5. Neither the firer nor his rifle should be touched. [I.T., 10 (5).]
6. The firer should not be told anything; if necessary he should be made to reason out the causes and remedy for failure by questions.
7. A minimum of interference on the part of the instructor when the recruit is actually firing. Any criticism should be made after the shot has been fired.

FIELD PRACTICES.

In field practices targets must be looked upon as an actual enemy, and service conditions must be observed. [M.R., 550.]

The effect of the enemy's fire and the nervous tension which it causes is absent, therefore results are better than can be expected in war. [M.R., 560.]

Quick opening of fire and effect from the first shot is essential. [M.R., 419, 548, 509, 523, 564.]

Targets which fall when hit add interest. [M.R., 547, 549.]

The object of the practice and the special lessons to be brought out should be explained beforehand. [M.R., 527, 553.]

No interference (except for safety) during the practice. [M.R., 530, 550.]

Full criticism of good and bad points on completion. [M.R., 527, 563.]

Ammunition in excess of that to be used should be issued to practice men in looking after it and in recharging the magazine whenever possible.

INDIVIDUAL FIELD PRACTICES.

Individual skill produces decisive effect at close ranges.

In range practices the soldier has applied practically some of the lessons of elementary training. He should have confidence in his shooting and know the peculiarities of his rifle at known ranges up to this limit of individual fire. [M.R., 503.]

Conditions have been comparatively easy, and he must apply his knowledge in firing at difficult service targets at unknown range. [M.R., 506, 507.]

Practical use of the following additional elementary points brought in :—
1. Use of ground.
2. Location of low service targets.
3. Choice of targets.
4. Judging distance.

5. Quick opening of fire.
6. Application from observation (partly practised in snapshooting).
7. Choice of rate.
8. Mutual assistance. [M.R., 509.]

High scores in range practices bear no relation to results of firing under service conditions, even in peace time. [M R., 504, 419.]

Distance, not over 600. Practices progressive as regards targets, distance, &c. [M.R., 529, 543.]

For examples, *see* Appendix.

Separate target for each man. [M.R., 524.]

Men fire in pairs; one fires, the other observes. Observer should not use field glasses. In later practices men may fire singly to bring out necessity for self-reliance. [M.R., 524, 526.]

Firers of each detail should be regarded as a squad. [M.R , 530.]

Markers are used to signal hits, or falling targets may be used. [M.R., 526.]

Men of a section should mutually assist each other. [M.R., 524, 526.]

Key ranges, over 600, may be given sometimes to bring out their use. [M.R., 528.]

Movement of firers and targets must be included. [M.R., 524.]

Skill in snapshooting and rapid firing must be increased. [M.R., 508, 525.]

Practice necessary in snapshooting standing during a *rapid advance*. [M.R., 515.]

Points for criticism:—
Loading at first safe opportunity; use of safety catch; selection of point from which to fire; method of advance to fire position; use of cover on position; watch on front; consultations as to range of objects useful as range marks; consultation as to wind; on targets appearing, consultation as to range and point of aim; quickness in opening fire; instant reloading; methods employed in firing at a target advancing; quickness in gaining effect; points of elementary training, both firer and observer; observer's power of observation and of reporting strike of bullet; method of correction for next shot; information given to rest of squad; rate of fire used; recharging of magazine.

COLLECTIVE FIELD PRACTICES.

Beyond 600 fire effect can only be assured by means of collective fire. [M.R., 505, 269; I.T., 116 (7) (iii).]

Collective field practices primarily intended to give all commanders practice in their duties of fire direction and control. [M.R., 523, 544, 542, 540, 510.]

Also gives practical experience in use of fire and its effects on various targets. Practice to men in applying what they have learnt in fire discipline. [M.R., 542, 510.]

Fire direction, control, and discipline often neglected at training with blank ammunition, therefore ball ammunition must be used to show their importance. [M.R., 511, 541; I.T., 107 (10).]

Collective field practices should be fired over 600 yards. [M.R., 543.]

APPENDIX.

TESTS OF ELEMENTARY TRAINING.

The following tests are essential. For method of conducting, see M.R., Sec. 64.

Oral Tests:
1. Care of arms and ammunition.
2. Description of natural objects.

Inspection:
1. Firing positions.

Standard:
1. Adjustment of sights (as laid down).
2. Regulation aim. To be tested from aiming rest; two aims out of the three must be correct.
3. Trigger pressing. Aim corrector and aiming disc: three out of three correct.
4. Rapidity of aim (as laid down).
5. Rapidity of loading (as laid down).
6. Rapidity of firing (as laid down).

MUSCLE EXERCISES.

The following will be performed as a 4th muscle exercise; bayonet to be fixed:—

Standing Load:

On guard.—Assume the correct " on guard " position.

Aim.—Assume the correct aiming position by advancing the right foot, align the sights and take the first pressure.

Note.—The words " On guard " and " Aim " will be repeated at intervals of 4 seconds.

Unload:
As before.

Practice II, Rapid Fire Training, can also be carried out as an additional muscle exercise in all positions.

RAPID FIRE TRAINING.

To be carried out in all positions with bayonets fixed, either as a separate exercise or during firing instruction when sufficiently advanced.

Practice I—(Clean and quick loading).

Command.	Points to note and criticise.
LOAD or STANDING—KNEELING—LOAD.	All movements carried out correctly and smartly. Magazine charged in one clear motion. Pouch rebuttoned. Safety catch applied. Firm grip with both hands. Eyes on target; but it is permissible to glance down to insert charger.
(Safety catches forward.) RE-LOAD. Repeat 5 times at intervals of one second. LOAD with another charger and repeat. REST or ORDER ARMS.	Instant opening and closing of breech in one movement. Bolt withdrawn to full extent each time. Correct grip with right hand as soon as breech is closed. Safety catches applied.

25

Practice II—(Reloading at shoulder and first pressure).

LOAD.	As in Practice I.
AIM.	Safety catches forward. First pressure taken.
RE-LOAD.	Rifle kept in shoulder.
As in Practice I, but given at intervals of 2 seconds.	First pressure only taken.
	Firm grip.
	Correct position of butt in shoulder.
	Cheek on butt, and head kept still as possible.
REST or ORDER ARMS.	Safety catches applied.

Practice III—(Rapid fire).

Not to be practised until Snap shooting has been taught.
Rifles and dummy cartridges to be carefully inspected.
Section in 2 ranks 10 paces apart facing inwards and extended to 2 paces. One rank fires, the other, provided with aiming discs if possible, checks. The instructor will himself continually check with the aiming disc.

LOAD.	All points as in Practices I and II; also—
5 or 10 rounds.	Accuracy and rapidity of aim.
RAPID FIRE.	Trigger pressure.
(Change over and repeat.)	Time.

Aids to rapid fire:

(1) Action "bright clean" and slightly oiled.
(2) Vice-like grip with left hand.
(3) Correct grip with right hand.
(4) Tilt rifle slightly to right when reloading.
(5) Keep head still.
(6) Count the number of rounds.

MINIATURE RANGE COURSE.

Practice on the miniature range should commence as soon as the recruit can assume a good prone position, aim with accuracy, and press the trigger; it should be spread over the period of elementary training which precedes range practices.

The following practices are suitable for cavalry, yeomanry and infantry recruits: R.E., R.A. and A.S.C. units should fire Part I and other selected practices as time permits.

General Instructions:

1. Firing will take place under the personal superintendence of a fully qualified officer, who will ensure that all the conditions are strictly observed and that the timing is accurate.

An instructor will supervise and instruct each firer.

2. Men who fail in any practice in Part I will repeat as often as the musketry officer thinks necessary, before passing to Part II.

3. In snapshooting practices the targets will be operated by a marker, under the direction of the superintending officer, who will be out of view of the firers.

4. Marking should be carried out from the firing point by means of field glasses.

5. If a jam occurs during a timed practice, rounds already fired will be disregarded, and the whole practice repeated.

6. It is advisable not to fire more than two practices in one day.

7. After completing Part II practices 6, 9, 10 should be repeated in box respirators.

PART I.

Distance 25 yards. 5 rounds to be fired in each practice.

No.	Practice.	Target.	Instructions.	Standard.
1	Grouping	2nd Class Elementary 200-25 (No. 32)	Lying with wrist or rifle rested.	3 inch group.
2	Grouping	2nd Class Elementary	Lying	3 inch group.
3	Application	2nd Class Fig. 200-25 (No. 36)	Lying	12 points.
4	Application	2nd Class Fig.	Kneeling	10 points.

PART II.

Distance 25 yards. 5 rounds to be fired in each practice.

No.	Practice.	Target.	Instructions.	Standard.
5	Grouping	2nd Class Elementary	Lying	3 inch group.
6	Application	1st Class Fig. 400-25 (72)	Standing in a trench if available; otherwise kneeling.	12 points.
7	Snapshooting	2nd Class Fig.	Lying over cover Target exposed for 5 seconds.	10 points.
8	Rapid Fire using ·22 rifle magazine and adapter or Hiscock Parker magazine.	1st Class Fig.	Lying 35 seconds allowed.	12 points.
9	Snapshooting	No. 3 Fig. 200-25 (88)	Standing in a trench if available. 4 seconds exposure	3 hits.
10	Rapid	No. 3 Fig.	Standing in a trench if available. 35 seconds.	3 hits.

The numbers in brackets refer to D.F.W. Contract Circular, 611.

PART III.

Individual and Collective Field Practices, framed so as to bring out the Competitive Spirit.

Examples :

Practice.	Targets.	Rounds.	Instructions.	Criticisms.
1. Individual ..	Fig. 3's held in cleft sticks against sand or sawdust bank.	5	Men work in pairs one fires and one observes.	1. Points of elementary training. 2. Observation and how result was communicated. 3. Alterations made as result of observation.
2. Individual ..	Any small targets that will fall or break when struck, with sand or sawdust back ground, two for each firer.	5	Men standing behind firing point; on order "Boche" double to firing point, seize rifles, load, &c. First man to knock both his targets down wins.	1. Rapidity of movement, assuming firing position, loading, &c. 2. Points of elementary training. 3. Time taken to open fire and obtain 2 hits.
3. Collective (knock-out)	8 targets as in No. 2 placed in two groups, and targets 12 inches apart.	5	Teams of 4 with a leader each opposite a group of targets. On order "Boche" as in Practice II. Time 1 minute. Casualties will not be simulated.	I and II as in Practice II. Rapid and accurate marksmanship.
4. Collective (Fire orders)	Targets suitable for concentrated, distributed or rapid fire.	10	Targets exposed as Superintending officer may direct. Inter-Section Competition.	1. Fire discipline. 2. Fire orders and control. 3. Description and rate of fire employed.

DEMONSTRATIONS.

Applicable to training in Parts i, ii, and iii may be fired, where the points they bring out best fit into the general programme, *e.g.* :—
1. The trajectories of various ranges: by poles, tapes showing angles of descent and searching power of bullets; and by using " tracer " ammunition.
2. The use of ground and cover: by individuals and sections; penetration of bullets into common substances
3. Firing with and without respirators adjusted.
4. Rapidity and accuracy of fire with British and German rifles.
5. Concentrated and distributed fire with " tracer " ammunition.
6. Rifle and Lewis Gun fire contrasted at various targets.
7. The value of oblique and enfilade fire compared with frontal.
8. The vulnerability of formations.
9. The A.R.A. Competition; and Platoon in the attack.

SUITABLE INDIVIDUAL AND COLLECTIVE FIELD PRACTICES.

GENERAL NOTES.

1. In practices No. 1, 2, 3, 4, and 6 five extra rounds will be issued to each firer. This is with the object of ensuring that men re-charge and to accustom them to looking after their ammunition in Battle.

2. All practices will be carried out in " Fighting order," which, for purposes of these practices is as follows:—
   Equipment as issued.
   Steel helmets.
   Respirators in the " Alert " position.
   Filled haversack.
   Filled waterbottle.

3. Bayonets will be fixed throughout all the practices.

4. In all practices. except Nos. 9 and 10, an instructor will be detailed behind every 2 firers, to note good and bad points. The instructor will on no account speak to or interfere in any way with the firers till the conclusion of the practice, unless to ensure their safety.

5. There will be no talking behind the firing line, but great training value can be obtained by onlookers who should discuss the practice in a low tone of voice.

6. Greater value and efficiency will be derived from these practices by rehearsal of each practice on the part of the men prior to carrying them out and by demonstration by instructors.

7. Interest will be stimulated by carrying these practices out as competitions.

No.—1. Individual practice.
Name.—" Down the range."
No. of rounds.—10 per man.
Targets.—1st class figure, one per firer.
Range.—500 to 100 yards.
Object and lessons illustrated.—(a) Fire combined with movement.
(b) To ensure and confirm the soldier in the knowledge of his rifle and its sighting elevation.
(c) Use of the rifle—bullet and bayonet.
(d) Fire discipline.
Notes and method of conducting.—(a) Individual exercise, but to be carried out by Sections.
(b) No time limit.
(c) Each firer will advance down the range from 600 to 100 yards and fire two rounds, and only two, at each fire position, viz.:—500, 400, 300, 200 and 100 yards. At 300 and 200 yards the kneeling position will be adopted: at other distances any suitable position may be used.

Bayonet sacks for each firer will be placed in an irregular line at each of the following points:—10 to 15 yards in rear of the 200 and 100 yards fire positions

(d) Rifles will be carried at the " trail " till within about 40 yards of the rows of sacks. The command " charge " will be given by the section commander on reaching a point within 10 to 20 yards of the sacks, when sacks will be bayoneted.

(e) The commands "Advance," "Charge," "Halt," will be given by the section commander.

(f) Points for criticism:—
  (a) Accuracy of fire.
  (b) Correct use of the bayonet.
  (c) Individual fire discipline.

(g) Highest possible score = 40 points. Standard score = 20 points.

Marker's Notes.—Targets to remain up till conclusion of practice. Each shot to be signalled quickly.

No.—2. Individual practice.
Name.—"Hurry down the range."
No. of rounds.—10 per man.
Targets.—1st class figure, one per firer.
Range.—500 to 100 yards.
Objects and lessons illustrated.—(a) The four lessons enumerated in No. 1.
(b) Rapid movement, before and after firing.
(c) Physical fitness.
(d) General speeding up.

Notes and method of conducting.—(a) See No. 1 notes (a) to (g), excluding note (b).

(b) Time limit imposed, to vary according to condition of range used, *i.e.*, more time for shingle than grass range. Normal time limit, one minute for each advance of 100 yards and firing two rounds.

(c) A pause of 15 seconds, indicated by a whistle blast, at the end of each minute to permit men to prepare for advance to next fire position, *i.e.*, adjustment of sights, re-charging, safety catch and preparing to advance.

(d) Timing of practice by Officer conducting.

Marker's Notes.—Targets to remain up till conclusion of practice. No shots to be signalled during the practice.

No.—3. Individual practice.
Name.—"Sniping."
No. of rounds.—5 per man.
Targets.—Figure No. 3, one per firer.
Range.—200 yards.
Object and lessons illustrated.—(a) Acting on his own.
(b) Concentration of mind.
(c) Alertness.
(d) Patience.

Notes and method of conducting.—(a) Firing round cover, or through a properly constructed loophole.
(b) Total time for practice, 8 minutes.
(c) Firers remain on the alert, at the aiming position, for 8 minutes and fires whenever his own target appears.

Prior to commencing practice, exact front to be watched by each firer should be indicated.

(d) Points for criticism:—
  (a) Position.
  (b) Watching his front.
  (c) Accuracy of fire
  (d) Points of elementary training.

(e) Highest possible score = 15 points. Standard score = 9 points.

Marker's Notes.—(a) Careful control of targets necessary, use a stop watch if available.

(b) Each target to be exposed 5 times only during the 8 minutes.

(c) Not more than 2 targets will be exposed at any one time.

(d) Each exposure to be for 3 seconds.

(e) The exposures to be at irregular intervals of time.

(f) Each target will be exposed in a different place each time within a lateral space of 3 or 4 yards according to number of firers and space available.

(g) Two exposures to be in rapid succession, i.e., up for 3 seconds, down for 1 second, up for 3 seconds.

(h) The fifth exposure of each target to be in the eighth minute; to ensure concentration of firer for the whole time limit.

(i) Hits will not be signalled till conclusion of practice.

No.—4. Individual practice.
Name.—" Firing in pairs."
No. of rounds.—5, per man.
Targets.—Collapsible: Iron falling plates, tiles or bricks; 5 for each firer.
Range.—Between 200 and 150 yards. Fire position to be off the normal firing point, if possible.
Object and lessons illustrated.—(a) Mutual assistance.

(b) Observation of fire and methods of indicating strike of bullets.

Notes and method of conducting.—(a) No time limit.

(b) Men of section work in pairs, close together.

(c) One firer fires his 5 rounds in succession, comrade observes for him and *vice versa*.

(d) Points for criticism:—
  (a) Points of elementary training.
  (b) Determining point of aim.
  (c) Observation of fire, exact, not vague information, *i.e.*, a bit high, a little bit right.
  (d) Mutual assistance.

(e) Scoring, 3 points per hit, highest possible score, 30 points per pair.

Marker's notes.—Targets placed in any convenient position where observation of strike of bullet is possible to the firers. Targets to be at least one yard apart.

No.—5. Individual practice.
Name.—"Assault practice."
No. of rounds.—5 per man.
Targets.—Figure No. 2 or 3; one per firer.
Range.—200 to 50 yards.
Object and lessons illustrated.—(a) Use of the rifle—bullet and bayonet.

(b) Firing standing.

(c) Rapid opening of fire.

(d) Assault training.

Notes and method of conducting.—(a) Individual exercise, but carried out by sections.

(b) Advance is assumed to be over broken, heavy, or uphill ground.

(c) Targets, one per firer, exposed at irregular intervals of time, 5 seconds each exposure.

(d) Officer conducting practice to regulate exposure of targets by signal or other means.

(e) After completing the 5 exposures, each firer will charge and bayonet 3 sacks, placed in three irregular lines, about 5 yards distance between lines.

(Four inch paper discs fastened to sacks).

(f) Points for criticism:—
  (a) Quickness in opening fire.
  (b) Accuracy of fire.
  (c) Correct use of bayonet.

(g) Scoring: 3 points per hit, 2 points per disc pierced. Highest possible score, 21.

Standard score, 15.

Marker's notes.—Targets to be exposed immediately each time a short ring or other signal is given from the firing point.

Regulate correct height of targets before practice commences.

No.—6. Section practice.
Name.—"Gas defence."
No. of rounds.—5 per man.
Target.—One screen, 6 feet long, 2 feet high, to be coloured brown or green or some natural colour, without aiming marks.
Range.—200 yards.
Object and lessons illustrated.—(a) To accustom men in quickly adjusting respirators and in firing with them on.
(b) Accuracy of fire.

Notes and method of conducting.—(a) Fired from a trench, rifles loaded and sights adjusted before commencement of practice.

(b) Time limit of one minute from command "Fire." Respirators to be adjusted after the command "Fire."

(c) Points for criticism:—
  (a) Adjustment of respirators.
  (b) Accuracy of fire.
  (c) Points of elementary training.

Marker's notes.—Screen to be placed in a position where observation of strike is possible.

No.—7. Section practice.
Name.—"The War Shot" or "Team Tile Competition."
No. of rounds.—10 per firer, *i.e.*, 5 rounds per firer per heat.
Targets.—Collapsible, iron falling plates, tiles or bricks, one per firer.
Range.—200 yards.
Object and lessons illustrated.—(a) Fire combined with movement.
(b) Alertness.
(c) Rapid loading and aiming.
(d) Importance of effect of first shot.

Notes and method of conducting.—(a) Teams to be of equal strength.
(b) Rifles unloaded and at safety.

(c) Time limit from command "Advance," one minute. Officer conducting practice to regulate the time.

(d) On the command "Advance," teams will double from the 300 to 200 yards fire position, load and open fire.

(e) Winners decided as follows:—
  (a) When all targets opposite one team are down first.
  (b) Team with most targets down when all rounds have been expended.
  (c) Team with most targets down at end of time limit.
  (d) In case of a tie in (c), team with most ammunition unexpended wins.

(f) Knock-out competition throughout party.

(g) Points for criticism:—
  (a) Speed.
  (b) Accuracy of fire from observation.
  (c) Team work.

Marker's notes.—Targets placed in a convenient position, at least one yard apart, where observation of strike of bullet is possible.

No.—8. Section practice.
Name.—"Superiority of Fire."
No. of rounds.—10 per man.
Targets.—Figure No. 3. One per firer, according to strength of section.
Range.—200 yards.
Object and lessons illustrated.—(a) Rapidity and accuracy of fire.
(b) Mutual support, rapid change of point of aim.
Notes and method of conducting.—(a) The section will be extended and in position on firing point, rifles loaded, sights adjusted; fire to be opened when targets appear.

(b) Fire will cease—
  (1) Should the number of targets up exceed the number of firers.
  (2) If all targets are down.
  (3) One minute after the first appearance of the targets.

(c) The time in which all targets are hit, or the number of targets left up at the end of a minute, should be noted.

(d) Points for criticism:—
  (a) Quickness in opening fire.
  (b) Accuracy of fire.
  (c) Mutual support.

Marker's notes.—(a) Careful control of targets necessary.

(b) On the signal to "Commence" being given, the number of targets ordered will be raised, about three paces apart. Ten seconds after two more targets will be raised, and two more every ten seconds, up to 50 seconds.

(c) Targets will be lowered when hit.

(d) If at any time all targets up have been hit, no more will be put up.

No.—9. Two sections.
Name.—"Mutual Support." Attack by two sections (one leader and six men).
No. of rounds.—15 per man.
Targets.—Two screens, *see* practice No. 6.

Range.—600 to 150 yards or 400 to 150 yards, according to ground available.

Object and lessons illustrated.—(a) Fire and movement.

(b) Use of ground.

(c) Moving by bounds.

(d) Mutual support.

(e) Fire discipline.

Notes and method of conducting.—(a) To be fired on a field firing range if possible, otherwise Classification range.

(b) Sections extended, intervals between sections at least 40 paces, but according to ground.

(c) Fire positions studied and roughly indicated before advance commences.

(d) Sections advance by alternate rushes from fire position to fire position.

(e) Length of bound dependent on ground.

(f) The fire of one section should be the signal for the other section to advance.

(g) For purposes of economy of ammunition, two rounds only will be ordered by section commanders at each opening of fire.

(h) Points for criticism:—
    (a) Fire positions.
    (b) Use of ground.
    (c) Mutual support.
    (d) Fire orders.
    (e) Fire discipline.

Marker's notes.—Two screens as far apart as possible, placed in a general line on a convenient position.

The number of hits to be recorded.

No.—10. Platoon practice.

Name.—"Platoon Competition."

No. of Rounds.—20 per rifleman, 3 magazines per Lewis Gun (if any).

Targets.—Four screens, see practice, No. 6.

Objects and lessons illustrated.—(a) Final advance, assault, occupation of final objective and repulse of the counter attack.

(b) Efficiency in the use of the rifle and Lewis Guns (if any).

(c) Fire and movement.

(d) Volume and rates of fire, and its application in attack and defence.

(e) Fire control and fire discipline.

Notes and method of conducting.—(a) The platoon will consist of 4 rifle sections, 2 of which may be armed with 1 L.G. each.

(b) This practice will be carried out by the whole platoon at once, if possible; if ground does not permit of this, by pairs of sections or by sections.

(c) There will be 2 fire positions, not less than 100 yards between the 2 positions selected.

(d) Three rows of bayonet sacks, one per rifleman, in each row, fitted with 4 inch discs will be placed on the ground in an irregular line as follows:—
    (a) About 15 yards in rear of the 1st fire position.
    (b) Midway between the 2 fire positions.
    (c) About 15 yards in rear of the 2nd fire position.

(e) The platoon or section will lie down, extended to at least 2 paces, 50 yards in rear of the first fire position, load with 5 rounds, sights adjusted. Sections armed with L.G. (if any) on the flanks.

(f) Platoon and section commanders may use their bayonets but will NOT fire.

(g) On a signal from the superintending officer, the platoon commander will give the order to " Advance." Sections will advance at a steady double, the Nos. 1 and 2 of the Lewis gun sections (if any) about 10 yards behind and covered by the remainder of these sections.

When about 15 yards from the first row of sacks, the order " Charge " will be given by the leaders, sacks will be bayoneted, and the fire position will be immediately occupied. Orders for the opening of fire will be given. (Riflemen, 5 rounds, Lewis guns 1 magazine each.)

(h) $1\frac{1}{2}$ minutes allowed from signal " Advance " by the superintending officer to the whistle blast, denoting the conclusion of the time limit.

(i) A pause of 15 seconds after the whistle blast, will be allowed for, reloading, adjustment of sights and safety catches.

(j) At the end of the 15 seconds' pause, the superintending officer will give the signal for the advance to be resumed.

After charging and bayoneting the second and third rows of sacks in succession, the platoon will occupy the second fire position. The leaders will order Rapid fire to be opened. (Riflemen, 15 rounds, Lewis guns (if any) **2** magazines each.)

(k) $1\frac{3}{4}$ minutes after the second signal to advance, the superintending officer will blow a whistle to denote the conclusion of the time limit. Total time for whole practice = $3\frac{1}{2}$ minutes.

(l) Scoring: Each hit on the screens = 1 point. Each disc pierced correctly with the bayonet = 2 points.

(m) Deductions: For every round fired after the conclusion of the whistle blasts, denoting " cease fire " = 2 points per round.

Bad control on the part of the platoon or section commanders during advances, lack of style or dash, incorrect use of the bayonet = 1 or more points up to a total of 3 per bayonet man.

(n) The following superintending officers are advisable when possible:—

1 officer to deduct points for rounds fired after the " whistle blasts," and generally to superintend practice.
1 officer or N.C.O. to count hits on screens.
1 officer or N.C.O. timekeeper.
1 officer or N.C.O. to check discs.
1 officer or N.C.O. P. & B.T. Staff when possible for judging style, &c.
1 N.C.O. register keeper, to write down number of discs pierced and deductions for lack of style and dash.

Marker's notes.—Screens to be placed in a general line, in a convenient position.

There will be a space of at least 3 feet between screens.

Note.—This practice may be fired with or without the inclusion of 1 or 2 Lewis guns, according to the conditions and facilities existing in the unit.

IMPROVISATIONS FOR "OUT OF THE LINE" TRAINING.

Subject.	Appliances Necessary.	How Improvised.
Aiming Instruction. Firing Instruction. T.O.E.T. ...	(a) Aiming Rests. (b) Targets ... (c) Eye Disc ... (d) Dummies ...	(a) Two filled sandbags; Trench; folded greatcoat. (b) Pioneer Sgt.: paint Bosche Head on ration box (see 30^x range below). (c) Inky cork will make bullseye on F.S. Postcard, perforate with pin. (d) A few may be made by sand-papering empty cases and inserting wooden plugs similar in shape to bullet, plug should be long enough to reach base of cartridge. For rapid loading practice use ball ammunition on 30^x range. For rapid loading practice with ball, off the range, insert three ball cartridges behind the trigger. Needs very strict supervision. To practice rapid fire with ball on 30^x range or against suitable bank, tie leather boot lace twice round rear end of striker.
Aiming Instruction. Firing Instruction.	(e) Artificial Cover. (f) Fatiguemen. (Aiming off for Wind and Movement).	(e) Trench or sand bag walls of varying heights. (f) Men of Section.
Judging Distance.	(a) Natural Objects. (b) Fatiguemen (c) Rangefinder (d) Large Scale Map.	(a) No improvision necessary, use trees, stumps, &c., for Unit of Measure. (b) Men of Section. (Appearance.) (c) On Regimental charge.
Visual Training	(a) Silhouettes (b) Fatiguemen	(a) Pioneer Sgt.: can make from ration boxes. (b) Men of Section. If blank needed, extract bullets from ball cartridges.
Indication and Recognition.	(a) Landscape Target. (b) Open Country.	(a) Double page picture from *Graphic*, &c. Railway Posters.
Fire Orders ...	(a) Aiming Rest	(a) Trench or Sandbags—Pointer Staff.
Fire Discipline Training.	(a) Targets ... (b) Fatiguemen	(a) Screens made of empty sandbags— Silhouettes and sandbags make Dummy Screens. (b) Men of Section.

Improvisations for "Out of the Line" Training—*continued*.

Subject.	Appliances Necessary.	How Improvised.
Assault Training	(a) Bayonet Sacks.	(a) Ration sacks stuffed with grass, &c., supported by wiring pickets.
	(b) Sandbags	(b)
	(c) Cover for Consolidation.	(c) Trench, ration tins filled with earth, sandbags.
	(d) Targets	(d) Dummy Screens as for Fire Discipline Training.
30 Range	(a) Stop Butt	(a) 1. Sunken road or suitable hillside. 2. Quarry. 3. Ruins sandbagged or banked up with earth.
	(b) Targets	(b) 1. R.E.'s supply. 2. Pictures from periodicals. Newspapers with suitable aiming marks improvised. 3. Tiles, bricks, jam tins, empty cartridge cases (loopholes, &c.). 4. Ground Landscape, cardboard and paper cuttings. For targets and Reference Objects.
	(c) Supports for Targets.	(c) 1. Cleft sticks. 2. 9" strip of canvas with 1" at bottom turned up to form pocket, wire clip to hold top of target. 3. Tin frames supported on wire. 4. Disappearing Target Frame.
	(d) Coupling Rings.	(d) Pioneer Sgt.: will make from wire or cardboard.

Third Army Musketry Camp—20-12-17.

PART II.

THE REFRESHING OF THE TRAINED OR SEMI-TRAINED MAN.

Notes for Instructors.

GENERAL METHOD.

The complete system of recruit instruction as given in Part I. is inapplicable when dealing with trained or semi-trained men.

The instructor must endeavour to find out as quickly as possible in what particulars his section is weak; he will then give such brief instruction from Part I. as may be necessary to correct these faults, and will afford his section ample practice to overcome them.

The general method of recruit instruction will be reversed, and the system employed will be that of:
"Test—Practice—Teach (where necessary)."

Instruction will be generally collective rather than individual: men will work by word of command, all movements as far as possible being carried out as a drill, and discipline must be tightened.

Detail will not be given except in the case of backward men.

Instructors will make every effort to inculcate the fighting spirit; training must be made as realistic as possible, all targets used should be Bosche figures, and all practices carried out with fixed bayonets.

Example:

FIRING INSTRUCTIONS.

1. *Trigger pressure.*—Test the section: if faulty give instruction as for recruit.
2. *Positions in open.*—Instructors must know the "Points to note": Plates xix. to xxv. M.R. No detail to be given. Minimum talk by instructor, maximum practice in handling the rifle by the men.
    (a) Inspect arms, pouches and dummies. Fix bayonets.
    (b) Extend section to 2 paces.
    (c) Point out targets. (Bosche figures).
    (d) "Load" or "Standing," "Kneeling," "Load."
        Men assume position, instructor checks.
        Note.—(If there are many serious faults, instructor may give the order "Rest," demonstrate with the rifle, followed by "Position," when men will return to the loading position).
    (e) "350" (or any suitable sighting elevation). Instructor checks.
    (f) "5 Rounds—Fire." Safety catch forward on number of rounds being named. Instructor checks faults during practice: (if they are very numerous, *see* note above; "Rest," demonstrate, "Fire").
    (g) "Cease Fire." Men recharge and await orders.

Muscle exercises will be carried out during the last 5 minutes: the instructor will extract the utmost smartness and perform the practices with his section until correct methods are acquired.

3. *Positions behind cover.*—All firing positions adapted to various kinds of cover. Faults checked. Correct methods explained and demonstrated if necessary.

Half the section act as targets and view the firers. Change over. Use of ground practised: demonstrated if necessary.

4. *Rapid loading and rapid firing.*—Test first: if backward carry out the exercises given in Appendix, Part I.

Example:

AIMING INSTRUCTION

The time allotted to each lesson depends on the hours available for musketry and the efficiency of the men when tested.

1. *Accuracy of aim.*—No preliminary detail of sights or rules for aiming, &c., will be given. The men's proficiency will be ascertained by the instructor checking their aims laid at the following targets:—
   (a) Bullseye with Bosche head, 100×.
   (b) Figure targets, 200-400.
   (c) Silhouettes, 200-600.
   (d) Ground and natural objects up to 600×.

Criticism and correction of faults (as for recruit) when they occur.

2. *Elevation.*—Test and impart a working knowledge of the Elevation table and aiming up and down by using—
   (a) Figure targets up to 400×
   (b) Silhouettes up to 600×

with marking discs to show supposed position of "last shot."

3. *Aiming off for* (a) *wind and* (b) *movement.*
   (a) A working knowledge of allowances tested and taught at—
       Figure targets up to 400×.
       Silhouettes up to 600×.
   (b) Allowances tested and taught at—
       Men up to 300×.

4. *Snapshooting*, carried out as a section exercise in two ranks. One rank fires, the other checks. The instructor will test each man.

Practice afforded by placing out men up to 300×, who give timed exposures.

Aiming at ground over 600× and aiming off for wind over 600×, can be dealt with during instruction in Indication and Recognition, Fire Orders, Fire Discipline Training, &c.

Example:

INTENSIVE TRAINING.

A method of carrying out training when only a short period of time is available.

The instructor or section commander will previously put the men through a brief test, which need not exceed half an hour, to discover in what particulars they are weak—*e.g.*, 10 minutes' firing instruction, during which he notes positions adopted, loading, bolt manipulation, sight setting, recognition of target, trigger pressing, and the elementary points of fire discipline generally. He should frequently change positions, target, range, rate of fire, &c. Five minutes asking questions on care of arms, and so on.

From the information thus gained a programme can subsequently be drawn up in which "hard" subjects (*i.e.*, those that require muscular exertion) and "easy" subjects (those in which men can sit or stand easy) are alternated.

The instruction in any subject it is found necessary to include in the programme should deal directly with the specific points in which the men have shown weakness.

Subjects.

"Hard."	"Easy."
Firing positions.	Care of arms.
Muscle exercises.	Aiming instruction.
Bolt drill.	Trigger pressing.
Rapid loading.	Visual training.
Rapid firing.	Judging distance.
Bayonet and assault training.	Recognition of targets.
Fire discipline and control exercises.	General knowledge.

Example of programme for one hour:—

Time.	Subject.
10 min.	Prone position. Slow and rapid fire. Check faults and demonstrate if necessary. Snapshooting, 5, 4, and 3 seconds exposure. Bolt drill, in loading and aiming positions.
5 min.	Care of arms. Instruction and catechism, confined to points in which section commander has noted carelessness or ignorance.
10 min.	Rapid loading. All positions commencing with prone. Where dummy cartridges are not available the trigger may be locked with three cartridges or cork and ball ammunition used.
10 min.	Recognition of targets (landscape target). Questions on aids to recognition. Orders for concentration and distribution of fire; men to indicate their point of aim. Visual training.
10 min.	Bayonet training; attack or defence as required. Preliminary assault course; bullet and bayonet course.
10 min.	Trigger pressing and elementary aiming.
5 min.	Muscle exercises.

To obtain full value from this method instructors must be very energetic and quick to detect and correct faults.

Example:

FIRE DISCIPLINE AND FIRE CONTROL EXERCISE.

A short exercise (15 min.) suitable for a platoon:—
1. The platoon commander can control the whole.
2. It practises the N.C.O.'s in commanding their fire units.
3. It combines fire control and fire discipline.

The platoon is formed into two ranks six paces apart. Two section commanders are told off as fire unit leaders on the flanks, one for the front rank, the other for the rear rank. Platoon commander acts as director of the exercise in the centre.

On the command " Advance " the platoon moves off at the trail. The commander gives the order " Standing," " Kneeling," or " Lying "—" Halt." The rear rank turns about and all assume the position ordered. Fire unit leaders double to the centre to control the fire of their respective units.

Platoon commander then orders "Concentrate" or "Distribute," when each fire unit commander will select his own target and give the necessary fire orders to his unit.

Faults will be checked.

Platoon commander orders "Cease Fire"; on the caution "Prepare to advance" the men will stand at ease, rear rank turns about, and fire unit leaders take post.

This can be repeated several times, changing the fire from concentrated to distributed; and where ground permits the direction can be changed.

Example:

QUICKENING EXERCISES.

To be carried out with ammunition on 30 yards or miniature ranges in all positions and from cover.

When fired on miniature ranges men will be told the sighting elevation required.

I.—*Competition*, between 2 firers or between 2 pairs of firers.

Targets, Figures 3, or any small targets that will fall or break when struck.

Method of conducting.—Firers standing at ease, rifles unloaded; on the word "Go" they load, adjust sights and fire.

The firer or pair of firers who knock their targets down first win.

II.—*Competition* between any number of firers, who will fire singly for safety.

Targets as in No. 1, six or as required.

Method of conducting.—Firer standing at ease, rifle unloaded; on the word "Go" he assumes prone position, loads, adjusts sights and fires 2 rounds; he jumps into a trench and fires 2 rounds; and then over the top and fires 2 rounds kneeling in the open.

Time limit, one minute, or less, according to proficiency.

The winner is the man who gets most targets down.

If ranges and ammunition are not available the following exercises are suitable.

I.—Section in two ranks 6 paces distant; front rank with aiming discs, prone, kneeling or standing as required; rear rank turned about, rifles on the ground with bolts and magazines out.

On the word "400—Go" each firer replaces bolt and magazine, loads with dummy cartridges, adjusts his sight, and in the position adopted by his front rank man fires 5 rounds at the eye disc.

The winner is the firer who gets the most accurate shots in the shortest time.

Front and rear ranks will change over.

The instructor must watch the firers very closely, and himself occasionally check the aims of the best men.

II.—Rapid loading competition. Dummy cartridges placed on the ground in chargers (number unlimited) $50^\times$ in front of the men.

On the word "Go" they double to their ammunition, and carry out loading and unloading as rapidly as possible in the prone position.

Time limit, one minute.

One half section to check the action of the other half; then change over.

The best man in each section can similarly compete to decide who is the best in the platoon or party.

III.—Rapid loading competition. The section will be divided into pairs. One man of each pair assumes loading position and is given 5 chargers of dummy cartridges. As fast as he loads and unloads the other man picks up the cartridges, replaces them in chargers and supplies the loader with ammunition.

If the loader can call "I am waiting" before he has loaded and unloaded 12 chargers, he wins.

On the contrary, if the other man of the pair can keep the loader supplied until he has loaded and unloaded 12 chargers, the other man wins.

The men of each pair then change over.

IV.—A section advances in single rank extended to one pace, rifles loaded and carried at the slope, trail, sling or high port, safety catches on.

A Boche figure is raised by signal, or fatigueman appears.

The instructor orders "Standing," "Kneeling," or "Lying"— "Aim": Each man will assume the position ordered as quickly as possible, align his sights and take the first pressure. As progress is made the instructor will merely caution the men what position to adopt at the next appearance of the target.

PART III.

THE TRAINING OF THE FIRE UNIT LEADER.
(S.S. 135 and 143).

	PAGE
Indication and Recognition of Targets	42
Theory of Collective Fire.—Atmospheric and other influences that affect elevation—beaten zones and how affected by ground.	43
Ranging.—Methods of determining sighting elevation : observation of fire.	45
Fire Orders.—For direction and control of fire under all circumstances: how given.	47
Methods of Practising Fire Orders.—With and without men ...	48
Fire Control Exercise with Men	49
Cover Ground and Formations.—To assist fire effect and prevent loss	50
Fire Action.—Principles of the application of fire : fire control and direction.	53
Training in the use of ground and Minor Tactical Exercises ...	56

THE TRAINING OF THE FIRE UNIT LEADER.

Fire effect depends less upon individual marksmanship than upon the fire direction and control exercised by commanders. Though discipline is the first essential of fighting power, even the best disciplined men are ineffective in war without properly trained leaders.

Platoon and section leaders must be made to feel their responsibility at all times, and be trained to exercise command. The issue of any fight is ultimately in their hands, and will depend upon their leadership and previous training.

The first essential in a leader is that he should possess power of command: this can be developed by acquiring the necessary knowledge; by cultivating a good word of command, and by insisting on the prompt obedience of his men; by studying their character, and by setting such an example himself in appearance and bearing as will gain their confidence and respect.

Every leader must be able to employ the fire of his unit to the best tactical advantage: to this end the following points are essential: —

1. He must be able to give clear, concise fire orders suitable for all occasions and targets, and exercise proper fire control over his unit.
2. He must cultivate an eye for ground, so as to quickly select fire positions, and be able to take advantage of good lines of approach that afford cover.
3. He must realise the close association of fire and movement, and know what formations to adopt in attack and defence, either to produce fire or in which to encounter it.
4. He must understand the theory of and the principles that govern the application of infantry fire.

In addition to the above "fire duties" there are others so intimately connected with leadership in battle that it is impossible to exclude them in training.

Situations will arise that call for the exercise of ingenuity and resource, opportunities must be afforded and schemes framed to develop these qualities.

Leaders must themselves be skilled men at arms, capable of leading and controlling their units in the assault; and they must realise that it is to them their men will look for that example of skill, courage, and determination which will always decide the issue of every fight.

INDICATION AND RECOGNITION OF TARGETS.

The System of Visual Training followed by the Commander is the Same as that laid down for the Private Soldier.

INDICATION.

Indication means the shortest and most easily understood description of an aiming point by a commander.

Indication and recognition necessary to ensure close grouping of collective fire. 75 per cent. of shots probably wasted owing to bad indication and recognition. [M.R., 532, 533.]

One system imperative in a battalion and throughout the Army. *Aiming points* must be described as seen with the naked eye. *A front* always to be pointed out, [M.R., 278.] if possible a definite point, and targets will be indicated as "slightly," "quarter," "half" right or left with reference to that point, the true angle being used in each case.

After change of direction a new front must be pointed out before indicating a target.

Taught in stages.

1st Stage.—Description of aiming points, without aids.

2nd Stage.—Description of different objects, using aids. [M.R., 279.]

Aids only used when absolutely necessary.

(a) *Reference points.*—Prominent objects, or others of military importance. Two hand-breadths apart. Reasonably distant. Of different kinds. Names by which they are known must be made clear to all.

(b) *Clock ray method.*—Shows the direction of an object from a reference point. Clock-face centred on the reference point. Direction right or left should be given before clock ray.

(c) *Finger breadth method.*—Shows roughly the distance of an object from a reference point. Only left hand should be used. Arm must be held straight out. Fingers vertical unless object is immediately above or below reference point; then horizontal. Reference point and object both kept in view. Necessarily inaccurate.

(d) *Combined method.*—(b) and (c) together, seldom necessary.

Practice in indication.—Key rifle laid on point to be indicated, or pin showing point on miniature landscape target, or point on landscape target actually pointed to. Officer or N.C.O. indicates point. Squad recognise it.

Test.

Unofficial.—Indication of four points. 80 per cent. of squad must recognise each.

THEORY—II.

1. This lecture, which deals with collective fire, has as its object the explanation of Sections 28, 29, 30, 31, 32, 33, and 35, Musketry Regulations, Part I.

All officers and N.C.O.'s must have a working knowledge of above.

Firing up and down hill.—[M.R., Sec. 28]. Only steep slopes have any great effect, viz., 20°, deduct $\frac{1}{8}$th of the range: 40°, deduct $\frac{1}{4}$: 60°, deduct $\frac{1}{2}$.

Atmospheric conditions.—[M.R., Secs. 29, 30]. Variations in barometric pressure are very small except where firing at considerable altitudes.

Only extreme changes of temperature require consideration.

Head and Rear Winds.—For strong winds increase or reduce elevation by 50^x at 1000^x range: by 100^x at 1500^x range.

2. Plate XII, M.R., represents a large target fired at by an individual, without alteration of sighting elevation or point of aim. Note the following points:—

(1) All the shots are not in the same place.
(2) The shot holes are more numerous in the centre.
(3) Approximately half the shots are above the centre horizontal line, the other half below.
(4) Approximately half the shots are on the right of the centre vertical line, the other half left.
(5) The distance from the topmost shot and the lowest one is greater than that between the extreme right and left shots.

From above we deduce the following:—
(1) Since shots are not in the same place, it follows that the trajectories of bullets do not coincide. The figure thus formed is known as the cone of fire.
(2) Since shot holes are more numerous in the centre we know that the cone of fire is denser in the centre than on the outside.
(3), (4) and (5) show us that the cone of fire is not circular but oblong in section, and that its density decreases uniformly from the centre to the outside.

3. Plate XIV, M.R., represents the size of rectangles which will contain the shots fired by an expert under the most favourable conditions, at a service target at different distances.

From this will be seen what a small chance even an expert has of hitting a prone figure at distances over about 600 yards. Compare the chances of the average shot firing, say, on a windy day, when he is tired or hungry.

4. Since we cannot expect fire to be effective over 600 yards when employed individually, we must use collective fire. Good illustration is the manual fire engine:—

The men working the engine represent the men of fire unit.
Water produced by their efforts represents stream of bullets.
Man holding the nozzle represents the fire unit commander.

Unless everyone works in conjunction no results can be hoped for.

5. Cone of fire from a number of rifles is larger than that from one, since skill varies, eyesight, &c. The size will be still further increased if firers are tired, aiming mark is hard to see, &c., &c.

6. Imagining that collective fire has been applied to a large vertical target marked with two concentric rings, and that a long mat has been laid out behind this target so as to collect all bullets passing through it.

That portion of the mat struck by all the shots passing through the target is known as THE BEATEN ZONE.

That portion of mat struck by shots passing through the centre ring is known as THE NUCLEUS OF THE BEATEN ZONE.

That portion struck by bullets passing through both the centre and larger ring is known as THE ZONE OF EFFECTIVE FIRE or EFFECTIVE BEATEN ZONE.

THE NUCLEUS contains 50 per cent. of shots fired.
THE EFFECTIVE BEATEN ZONE contains 75 per cent. of shots fired.
THE BEATEN ZONE 90 per cent. of shots fired.
The remaining 10 per cent. are too far out to be included.

7. Useful results can only be expected if the target is included within the EFFECTIVE BEATEN ZONE for any range.

Experiments have shown that as range increases the size of the EFFECTIVE BEATEN ZONE (E.B.Z.) decreases. This is due to increased angle of descent of bullet. Beyond 1,500 yards it increases again, especially laterally, owing to increased effects of errors in aiming, &c., &c.

Under favourable peace conditions it has been found that the size of the E.B.Z. varies very little when fired by different units.

Sizes of E.B.Z. on level ground are as follows:—
500^x—330^x long, 7' wide. 1,000^x—180^x by 14'. 1,500^x—150^x by 28'.

8. The permissible error in ranging is equal to half the depth of the E.B.Z. for any particular range, e.g.:—

Assume target to be 1,000 yards distant.
E.B.Z. for 1,000 Mark VII. is 180 yards.
If range is obtained absolutely correct, half E.B.Z. will be one side of target, half the other.
If error of over 90 yards is made (i.e., half E.B.Z.), whole of E.B.Z. will miss target.

9. Effect of slope of ground on the size of E.B.Z.

Most important for officers and N.C.O's. to realise effect produced by E.B.Z. falling on to ground which is not horizontal, since it will guide them in use of ground. Cover, and Formations (dealt with in separate lecture).

Musketry Regulations, Part I., paras 185 to 191, and plates XVII. and XVIII.

Night firing. [M.R., 197]

RANGING.

Ranging.—The means adopted for ascertaining the sighting elevation required to hit an object.

Range and *sighting elevation* are not always the same: when firing up or down hill; when barometric pressure and temperature are not normal; when a head or rear wind is blowing. [M.R., 169, 170, *et seq.*]

Necessity for ranging.—Errors in elevation cause greater loss of fire effect than personal errors in shooting at distances over 600 yards. If sighting is incorrect, the least effect will be obtained when shooting is best. [M.R., 302, 301; I.T., 116 (15).]

Principal methods of ranging:—
 (1) *Judging distance by eye.*—Most frequently used; has been fully dealt with. Average error about 15 per cent.
 (2) *Observation* of the strike of bullets, or of their effect on the enemy. [M.R., 301.]

The best means, but not always possible. [M.R., 330; I.T., 116 (16).]
Sufficient volume of fire must be employed to ensure observation. [M.R., 331.]

Short bursts of rapid fire often simplify observation. [M.R., 331; I.T., 116 (12).]

The fire must be closely grouped. [M.R., 331, 196.]

Objects in vicinity of target may be used to range on, for better observation. [M.R., 333.]

One elevation well under the estimated range should first be used. Beware of the few short or over shots. Bold alteration of sighting necessary. [M.R., 332; I.T., 116 (16).]

The best position for observation, above and behind the firers. [M.R., 334.]

(3) *Range-taking with instruments.*—Special courses must be held to ensure efficiency; inseparable from fire action; fully and practically trained range-takers invaluable; badly-trained and inaccurate range-takers dangerous; choice of range-takers, lance-sergeants or corporals; good and well-trained eyesight; strong; intelligent; good writing; good military vocabulary; able to write short, clear, descriptions; self-reliant; good map reading.

Other Methods of Ranging. [M.R., 301.]

Use of maps.—Generally too small scale; difficult to locate exact positions. [M.R., 319.]

Sound.—Count at rate of eleven beats in three seconds; each beat equals 100 yards.

Information from other troops.

Forward or back reckoning, after having obtained a range.

RANGE CARDS.

Preparation of range cards for attack.—Should always be used in attack; first objective is a line or point which is to be made good in the advance; need not be exact position of enemy; if first objective is over 2,000 yards, range-taker must either approach to within that distance or take preliminary key ranges. [I.T., 122 (4).]

Ranges taken in *direct* line of advance.

0	Description of first objective	2000 Very accurate
	(Unmistakable objects, described so that they will be recognised when reached).	
500	Row of fir trees	1500
1000	Hedge with pollarded trees	1000
1400	Wind pump	600

Preparation of range cards for defence.—(a) Mark off on card position from which ranges are taken; (b) describe position accurately; (c) select an unmistakable object and draw a *thick* setting ray to it; (d) draw two semi-circles representing the 600 and 1,000 yards limits; (e) select objects to range on—"range marks"—these should be positions, etc., which enemy will occupy or have to pass, or obstacles, e.g., bridge, gap in thick hedge, barbed-wire fence, &c.; (f) draw ray as accurately as possible to show direction of object, and of a length corresponding to the distance; keep card set; (g) write short descriptions (or draw representations) of the objects at the end of the ray; (h) write the distance to each object under the description; (i) avoid too many rays, which are apt to become confusing; (j) when possible, make one ray do for more than one object. [I.T., 102, 129 (3).]

All men to be made familiar with distances; pass to relieving troops. [I.T., 129 (3).]

LATERAL JUDGING DISTANCE. [M.R., 318.]

All officers, non-commissioned officers and scouts should know some measurement which will cover laterally one-tenth of a forward distance; measurement can be obtained by covering 10 yards at 100 yards, then applying at longer distances.

With the rifle held in the aiming position the back sight protectors of the S.M.L.E. approximately give this measurement.

FIRE ORDERS.

"*Fire Organisation*" *Orders* are issued by a commander to secure co-operation in the fire of various arms and units.

"*Fire Direction*" *Orders* given by an Officer or N.C.O. commanding more than one fire unit to their fire-unit commanders. [I.T., 123 (9).] Contain directions as to how the fire of units is to be used. [M.R., 281.]

Written, signalled, passed, or verbal. If passed must comply with I.T., 96 (3). [I.T., 119 (4).]

"*Fire Control*" *Orders* given by fire-unit commanders to their men, passed or verbal. If passed I.T., 96 (3) must be complied with. [I.T., 123 (10).]

"*Fire Unit.*"—The normal fire unit is the section, but it may be a platoon.

The only difference between a COMPLETE Fire Direction Order and the subsequent Fire Control Order is the addition of the Command "Fire" to the latter.

Signal to Commence.—Should the leader responsible for Fire Direction wish to keep the opening of fire in his own hands he will add the caution "Wait my Signal" to his order.

Fire Orders for *Concentrated* or *Distributed* fire, which only differ in the indication, may be:—
- (a) Normal.
- (b) Brief.
- (c) Anticipatory.

(a) NORMAL will be given in the following sequence:—
FIRE DIRECTION. (Number of Fire Unit, if necessary).

I. *Range*: (1) Once sights are adjusted, the men can concentrate their whole attention on recognizing the target from which they need not then look away.

(2) Knowledge of the range limits the area to be searched for the target.

II. *Indication*: for Concentrated Fire.

The point of aim must be given; this may be part of the actual target or an auxiliary aiming point, or a distance indicated from either.

When no special part of the target or auxiliary aiming point is mentioned, the centre of the lowest visible part is intended.

When an auxiliary aiming point is given, the target should seldom be mentioned as well.

For Distributed Fire.

The limits between which fire is to be distributed will be named. The extent of the target given should not exceed that of the unit firing. When a platoon frontage is given each section will distribute along the whole front.

III. *Number of rounds.*—Normally five, so as to ensure a lull in which fresh orders can be heard, and magazines recharged (M.R. 273).

(" Wait my signal," if necessary.)

FIRE CONTROL.

IV. *Fire* or *Rapid Fire.*

NOTE: If the platoon officer can make his orders heard by the men of his unit he will give I., II., III., IV. himself.

How fire orders should be given. [I.T., 11, 119 (4).]

CALMLY ; otherwise confusion.

WITH DECISION ; as orders, to command attention and obedience.

LOUD ; for everyone concerned to hear.

PAUSES ; to allow each part to be understood and acted on (or if necessary repeated).

Every word must be important. [M.R., 281.]

Avoid conversation ; unnecessary or confusing detail ; repetition of point of aim or sighting elevation. If no change is to be made after a pause (*e.g.*, 5 ROUNDS), " FIRE " may be sufficient.

Cease fire means reload and wait for orders. The whistle may be used to draw attention. [M.R., 284.]

Sighting best changed by UP or DOWN, 200, &c. [M.R., 283.]

Mutual understanding between commanders and their men simplify fire orders. [M.R., 282.]

(*b*) BRIEF orders may be necessary at obvious targets, *e.g.*,

" ¼ left, rapid fire."

" 400, ½ right, rapid fire."

(*c*) ANTICIPATORY orders may be given both in attack and defence anticipating movement either of one's own troops or those of the enemy : *e.g.*, " 400, No. i. Section is going to advance, when I give the order " fire," distribute fire along the trench "—" 500, quarter right, a copse. When the enemy comes out into the open, aim at the centre of his line and open rapid fire on my order."

In order to facilitate control outside decisive range, it is to be understood that in cases where the number of rounds is not given in a " fire control " order, the men should be trained, when reloading, to look to their section commander or nearest fire-unit commander, in case further orders are to be issued.

METHOD OF PRACTISING FIRE ORDERS.

Fire orders should be frequently written down and afterwards discussed.

Communicating instruction.—Fire-unit commanders are formed up not less than fifty yards apart. The instructor gives a fire order to one, which is repeated by each in turn ; the instructor checks the accuracy of the order as it is passed, and criticises the way in which it is given.

Control on men.—Concealed fatiguemen are called up individually and fire blank—meanwhile the squad (of N.C.Os.), except the commander, is turned away. The fatiguemen again take cover; the squad is turned about. The commander gives his fire orders—the squad adjust sights and lay rifles from rests on the point at which they would have fired. The fatigueman is again called up, aims and sights checked, and the distance taken with a range-finder. The fire orders and probable effect of fire are then criticised. As progress is made two fatiguemen may be called up at a time and orders given for distribution between the points which they mark.

Use of key rifles.—These may be laid on points instead of using fatiguemen; when using landscape targets pins may be used to show the points on the miniature.

Control on dummy screens.—Suitable for a squad or section. Fatiguemen with dummy screens may be concealed and called up when required. [M.R., Part II, Plate 31.]

They may be used to represent small bodies of infantry in various formations, according to the number of dummy screens used and their arrangement, *e.g.*—

A small body advancing in close formation.
A small body moving to a flank.
An extended line firing, or advancing.
A firing line being reinforced.

Other targets may be used either separately or together with dummy screens. [M.R., Part II, Plate 30.]

Note.—In all the above exercises, unless the targets obviously represent service targets, commanders should be told what they are supposed to engage, *e.g.*, in control on men, when a single man appears a commander might be told that a machine-gun is concealed at the point marked by the fatigueman. Only such fire as the supposed target justifies should be allowed.

Dummy screen exercises.—Suitable for one or more platoons. These are not tactical exercises, but are framed in order to practise commanders in giving fire direction orders, and fire-unit commanders in giving fire control orders. The suitability or otherwise of the orders should be discussed with reference to the nature of the targets, but without reference to possible tactical results. At first, direction orders must be given, and these must be accurately carried out by fire-unit commanders, the orders in each case being full and detailed under a variety of situations. As proficiency increases, direction orders should be curtailed to develop initiative and judgment in fire-unit commanders. The final object to be aimed at is the reduction of orders to a minimum without loss of control or effect.

FIRE CONTROL EXERCISE WITH MEN.

(Suitable as a Platoon Exercise.)

An instructional exercise, with no tactical consideration, for the teaching of Fire Orders, Fire Control, Passing of Orders, and Fire Discipline.

It can be carried out either in open country or on landscape targets. The former is, of course, best.

Open Country.

1st Phase.

1. Select a suitable piece of ground, giving good landscape in front.
2. Make up good fire orders; if possible, with assistance of one or two others. Each order should be framed to meet some imaginary situation.
3. Take ranges, or estimate distance as accurately as possible, to the various targets selected.
4. Choose exact position for each squad, so as to ensure that each target is visible to all.
5. Place squads in position, in line, about 10 paces between squads; the fire-unit commander kneeling behind his squad. As proficiency increases the squads can be placed further apart.
6. Give out the orders quietly to one commander, and have them passed from commander to commander along the line.
7. As a squad commander shouts the orders to the next commander, the men of his squad act on the orders.
8. After the orders have been given, commanders note how many men fired at correct target and other points as in fire discipline training.
9. General criticism by the directing officer.

2nd Phase.

1. Commanders are called together and told that a certain situation exists.
2. They return to their squads and give fire orders to meet that situation.
3. Either:—
   (a) Each commander writes down his orders before giving them, or
   (b) Each commander has behind him a man who writes down what the commander actually says.
4. This enables all the orders given to be afterwards criticised.
5. The original orders having been made up with a view to some definite situation existing, these situations can then be used in the second stage.

Landscape Targets.

1. The same general arrangements apply as for open country, but each squad must have a landscape target placed in front of it.
2. The landscape targets must all be the same picture.
3. Carry out as for open country, first and second stage.

COVER GROUND AND FORMATIONS.

Close connection between musketry and manœuvre. [I.T., 1 (10); 108 (1).]

Necessary to close with enemy to gain decisive victory. [I.T., 90 (2).]

All variations of combat, either attack or defence; impossible to lay down fixed system of either; general principles exist, these must be applied with common sense, according to ground and situation. [I.T., 114, 118 (1).] S.S. 143.

MEN must be individually instructed how to make proper use of cover of all kinds, they must be trained in elementary field craft and should know the thickness of common substances that are bulletproof.

SECTION LEADERS, minor leading; selection of small fire positions; an eye for ground; ability to spot covered lines of approach.

PLATOON COMMANDERS.—Reconnaissance; how fire is affected by ground; selection of fire positions with a view to fire effect and cover; best formations in which to encounter hostile fire.

COVER.

The soldier's first duty is to kill. Fire effect is the first consideration, cover second.

For method of instruction. *See* " Firing Instruction " in Part I.

Good cover should—
  (a) have a sufficient field of fire;
  (b) permit of the free use of the rifle;
  (c) be bulletproof;
  (d) be inconspicuous.

Bulletproof.

Earth (average), 3 ft. dry, 4 ft. wet. Clay, 6 ft. Brickends, gravel, shingle (between boards), 8 in. Sand, 2 ft. dry, 3 ft. wet. Sandbags (size varies), 2 headers, 3 stretchers.

Brickwalls, 9 in., rifle fire; 14 in., M.G. fire.

Wood—oak, 2ft. 6 in., fir, 4 ft. 6 in.

Cover from view only useful when enemy does not know it is occupied, otherwise it attracts fire; men lying in open will generally suffer less loss.

Advantages of cover.

Concealment during advance or whilst firing.

Protection from fire gives confidence.

Rest for rifle increases fire effect.

Disadvantages.

May delay advance and cause crowding.

May offer a good aiming mark.

May prevent free use of rifle.

May attract men out of direct line of advance, expose them to oblique or enfilade fire, and lead to loss of direction.

[I.T., 108-123 (11), 139 (5).]

Cover from aircraft.—[I.T., 108 (7), (8), 118 (11).]

GROUND AND FORMATIONS.

In the attack the advance will be assisted by:—
  (a) **Reconnaissance.** [I.T., 121, 122 (6).]
  (b) **Use of cover** ground and formations to produce fire effect and reduce loss. [M.R., 185.] [I.T., 103.]
  (c) **Fire action of all arms to assist movement.** (*See* Fire Action.)

Reconnaissance as thorough as time and circumstances permit.

The nature of the ground, flat or undulating; dead ground affording covered lines of approach; fire positions.

[I.T., 121 (4), 122 (4), 123 (3).]

May be effected by—

Actually going over the ground; studying it with glasses; maps.

Leaders must have a general knowledge of how beaten zones are affected by ground.

On forward slopes.—Depth of beaten zone is lessened as slope increases; shallow formations; successive lines may be closer. [M.R., 187, 188.]

Often best to make one rush down a long slope. [I.T., 121 (12).]

On reverse slopes.—Depth of beaten zone greatest when slope and trajectory are parallel; frequently swept by unaimed fire. [M.R., 189.]

Firing line on a crest.—On a very steep reverse slope; supports and reserves close up at all ranges. [M.R., 191.]

On a gentle reverse slope, supports far in rear when enemy at long range; close up in defiladed zone when enemy at short range. [I.T., 123 (7).]

In wooded country.—Successive lines may be closer.

Under artillery and long-range infantry fire.—Very small columns most suitable; sections in file or single file; facilitate use of ground and control; must be preceded by scouts; if surprised by artillery fire best to continue advance; this formation should be maintained as long as possible.

Under effective infantry and M.G. fire.—Deployment is necessary for two purposes—to produce fire and to diminish loss. Extension depends on volume required; fire effect chief consideration.

When checked by enemy's fire.—Advance by rushes. [I.T., 121 (12).]

Mutual support must be automatic between sections or platoons. [I.T., 123 (6).]

Rushes sudden and simultaneous; fire seldom opened between fire positions; advantage must be taken of unexpected bursts of covering fire from artillery, machine-guns, or specially detailed bodies of infantry, or friendly cavalry charges, &c. [I.T., 121 (16), 118 (8), 92 (5).]

At close infantry range.—All ground practically swept by fire; under heavy fire rushes necessarily shorter; covering fire and mutual support must be heavy; parts of line on favourable ground work forward; creeping, crawling, &c., exceptional; units must be re-formed under cover, and, if necessary, re-told off, so that control may be maintained. [I.T., 93 (11), 121 (12).]

Under machine-gun fire.—If caught in close formation take cover; extend on wide front if possible; use of cover, ground, and background; irregular advance by small groups; avoid ground favouring observation of fire; avoid aiming marks.

Against cavalry.—Protect flanks; steady timely fire; any formation suitable for effective fire; dead ground favours cavalry. [I.T., 118 (7).]

Defence.

Active defence only can be decisive. [I.T., 134, 126 (3).]

Positions should be organised in depth, and arranged chequerwise, so as to bring mutually supporting fire to bear.

Forward defensive positions not necessarily a continuous line. Short lengths of fire positions for sections mutually supporting one another by fire least conspicuous and have advantage of surprise. Behind them main line of resistance can be organised. [S.S., 143, 14 (1) (2) (3).]

CHOICE OF GROUND.—General position chosen for tactical reasons
Line to be held chosen to give maximum fire effect with least exposure to artillery fire.
Field of fire may be often sacrificed to latter. [I.T., 127 (1).]
Ground over which enemy must advance to be covered by direct or flanking fire or both. [I.T., 129 (1), (4), 116 (11).]
CLEARANCE OF FOREGROUND.—A clear field of fire, of at least 400 yards if possible. [M.F.E., 29; I.T., 129 (3).]
CONCEALMENT.—Avoid hill-tops and prominent salients. High-sited trenches facilitate reinforcing, &c., but often leave dead ground. [I.T., 129 (4), 140 (4).]
Fire plunging. [M.R., 167.]
Low-sited trenches facilitate concealment, grazing fire. Often impossible to reinforce. [I.T., 129 (4).]
Fire trenches. Parapet cannot be too low, if field of fire sufficient: eye must be brought to level of firer's eye when siting; must assimilate background; *sharp lines to be avoided.* [M.F.E., 29.]
OBSTACLES, WIRING.—Break up enemy's formations; force enemy to take most exposed lines of advance; delay enemy under close and particularly under flanking fire. [M.F.E., 42; I.T., 129 (5).]
COMMUNICATIONS AND COUNTER-ATTACK.—Necessary for free movement of defenders in rear of line held.
No possible means of keeping up communication should be neglected.
Commanders must be prepared to take the initiative.
Ground over which immediate counter-attacks will be made to be reconnoitred. [S.S., 143 (4), (5), (6), (7).]

FIRE ACTION.

Fire alone can seldom win a battle. Necessary to close with enemy to gain a decisive victory. Impossible to lay down fixed system of attack or defence. General principles exist, must be applied with common sense. [I.T., 90 (2); S.S., 143.]
To produce best fire effect, best use must be made of the ground occupied by both oneself and enemy, and of the knowledge of vulnerability of targets. [I.T., 118 (1); M.R., 185.]

ATTACK.

Principal uses of fire in attack:—
To assist advancing troops to get close to enemy. [I.T., 121 (6).]
To prepare the way for assault.
Fire seldom opened in attack when satisfactory progress can be made without it. [I.T., 116 (8).] But opportunities of inflicting loss on vulnerable targets must be taken full advantage of [I.T., 116 (7), 118 (9)] by platoon commanders.

COVERING FIRE.

Success or failure depends on the covering fire provided by (1) artillery; (2) machine guns; (3) specially detailed infantry; (4) mutual support between sections and platoons, with rifles and Lewis guns. Fire and movement being always in close association.

Defence.

Supply of ammunition being easier:—Fire may be opened at longer range than in attack to produce premature extension with loss of control and delay. Generally best for decisive results to wait. [I.T., 116 (9), (13).]

Collective Fire.

The fire of any number of rifles used under the orders of a leader is called Collective Fire. It may be either Concentrated or Distributed. Collective fire is used as long as possible [M.R., 270, 505, 273, 176]:—

(a) Keeps men in hand.
(b) Checks the expenditure of ammunition.
(c) Enables fire to be used to the best tactical advantage. [M.R., 505.]
(d) Gives best assurance of correct sighting and point of aim.
(e) Only means of surprise by fire.
(f) Gives best results.

The normal fire unit is the section; it may be sometimes a platoon.

Good fire effect cannot be produced without skilful fire direction by platoon commanders fire control by section commanders, and fire discipline on the part of the men.

The effect of collective fire depends upon:—

	Men.	*Fire Unit Leaders.*
(1) CLOSE GROUPING	Marksmanship. Recognition of target. Fire Discipline.	Good fire orders. Ability to control fire.
(2) FIRE DIRECTION...	*Officers.* Elevation and deflection. Regulation of volume. Choice of target and kind of fire employed.	

(1) Provided for in the preliminary training of men and fire unit leaders.

FIRE CONTROL.

Fire control includes all the duties of fire-unit commanders in handling the fire of their units according to "Fire Direction" orders. [M.R., 270; I.T., 116 (2), 123 (10).]

1. Carry out "Fire Direction" orders.
2. If "Fire Direction" orders have not been received, or are incomplete, they must act on their own judgment in deciding all necessary points. [I.T., 116 (2).]
3. Give "Fire Control" orders to the men.
4. Observation.
5. Supervise the men of their sections, and maintain fire discipline.

Means of controlling collective fire:—

(a) Naming number of rounds. [M.R., 273.]
(b) Passing of orders along firing line. [I.T., 96.]
(c) Signals. [I.T., 94.]
(d) Short whistle. [I.T., 95.]

(2) FIRE DIRECTION.

Fire direction includes all the duties of platoon officers, which are necessary to enable the fire-unit commanders under them to handle the fire of their units to the best tactical advantage.

M.R., 270, 185, 301, 523.
I.T., 116 (2), (6), 118, 119, 123 (3), (9), 129 (9).

ELEVATION.—The target must be in the effective beaten zone.
The distance of the target not necessarily the sighting elvation required.
Errors of the day (atmospheric), steep slopes, head and rear winds, may have to be allowed for.
Every effort must be made to verify the elevation by observation of the strike of bullets (*see* Ranging). This will not always be possible.

DEFLECTION.—The importance of giving approximately correct deflection in engaging narrow fronted targets with concentrated fire owing to small width of E.B.Z.
Wind allowances at $500^\times$: 2 ft. (mild), 4 ft. (fresh), 6 ft. (strong).
At $1,000^\times$ multiply by 5; at $1,500^\times$ by 10.
For indication of point of aim, *see* "Aiming Instruction."

REGULATION OF VOLUME.—Volume may be increased by: increasing the rate of fire; increasing the number of firers. Generally a question of rate. [I.T., 90 (3).]
Number of firers limited to one per yard. [I.T., 128 (3).]
Practical value of rapid fire: If opposing forces on equal front, the side using greatest volume with accuracy will win.

Deliberate fire.—The normal rate, five to six rounds a minute. [I.T., 116 (12); M.R., 274.]

Rapid fire.—The best rate of individuals. A reserve of power. [M.R., 275.]

15 rounds a minute, but varies with:—
{ the eyesight, training, and physical condition of the man; visibility of the aiming mark; the range. [M.R., 274, 273:]

Only used when the effect obtained in a given time with deliberate fire would not be sufficient. [I.T., 116 (12), 118 (9), 137 (4).]
Always used in short bursts, except in cases of emergency at very close range.

CHOICE OF TARGET AND KIND OF FIRE EMPLOYED.—Important that leaders should appreciate the principles of concentration and distribution in respect of the kind of fire ordered at any particular target.

Concentrated fire.—The dense beaten zone is effective against vulnerable and narrow-fronted targets, to produce decisive effect at a particular point and for ranging. Used at any range.

Distributed fire has a dispersed beaten zone, therefore no decisive effect. It can be used up to $1,000^\times$ to neutralise the enemy's fire, to cover or prevent movement, and at linear targets generally.

OBLIQUE AND ENFILADE FIRE.

More effective than frontal fire; usually a surprise. Larger target surface obtained. Against a long line, errors in ranging not so important if enfilade fire used. [I.T., 116 (11), 118 (9).]

Target normally will be that which is checking the advance, or is of the greatest tactical importance at the moment, but opportunities for employing oblique or enfilade fire should be taken full advantage of by Commanders; generally presented by targets ¼ and ½ right or left of one's fire position.

The fire action of the platoon is summarised in the following principles:—

(1) Cover all movement by fire. (Lewis guns and mutual support between sections.)
(2) Assist neighbouring platoons. (Opportunities for employing oblique and enfilade fire.)
(3) The judicious use of rapid fire. (Either when target justifies it or occasion demands it.)
(4) Obtain superiority of fire before delivering assault. (Enveloping tactics, converging fire, embracing enfilade and oblique.)

TRAINING IN THE USE OF GROUND AND MINOR TACTICAL EXERCISES.

The skilful combination of fire and movement is of the utmost importance in the infantry attack.

A study of this subject resolves itself fundamentally into a question of:—

(1) The use of ground,
(2) The adoption of suitable formations,
(3) The employment of the weapons.

In the earlier training of the fire unit leader these matters are more conveniently dealt with separately, but it is essential that they should be combined in later training.

During firing instruction he will have been taught the individual use of cover, how to modify his firing positions to suit various descriptions and heights of cover, how to rest his rifle properly, and avoid undue exposure: concurrently with this he will have been instructed during visual training in the elements of field-craft, *e.g.*, visibility as affected by movement, or background, the necessity of avoiding hill-tops, sky-lines, &c.

The exercises here detailed suggest the progressive sequence of training required to give a section commander that knowledge and practice that are necessary and without which he is not fit to be trusted with the handling of his men in the field: they should precede " the Minor Tactical Exercises (without men)."

In all practices of this nature the selection of suitable ground by the instructor is of great importance to bring out the particular lessons he desires to emphasise.

During the performance of these or similar exercises demonstrations of correct and incorrect methods should frequently be given. Where suitable ground is not available, or in wet weather, instruction can be given on sand models.

1st Exercise.—The individual stalk where front is unlimited.
Object.—To teach the use of ground.

Procedure.—A definite point is selected 200–400 yds. away where a sniper or point of a patrol is supposed to be located, the object is to approach sufficiently close to shoot with the certainty of killing. The section or party is given a few minutes to study the ground, to decide upon the position from where to take the shot and to consider the best means of getting there. Individuals may then be questioned, and one or more detailed to carry out the practice, if possible to exemplify both good and bad methods. The instructor and remainder of the class will proceed to the selected position to view the action of the stalkers, and will note faults committed.

Criticism.—On the conclusion the following points will be discussed:—

1. The reasons for the line of approach selected.
2. The fire position chosen.
3. If risks had to be taken, were they taken early while there was least chance of being seen and hit? or were they taken late?
4. Was full advantage taken of dead ground and cover both from fire and view?
5. Were sky-line, high ground, unsuitable back-grounds avoided?

2nd Exercise.—The section stalk, front unlimited.

Note.—Commanders will first be exercised in handling their Units from a drill point of view only, until simple battle formations. *e.g.*, the artillery and blob from column of route, movements into file, single file, extended order, change of direction, &c., can be rapidly carried out with precision.

Object.—To teach the use of ground and formations.

Procedure.—As in the first exercise a definite objective is pointed out 400–500 yds. away, and a few minutes are allowed in which leaders consider the problem and decide upon the following points:—

(a) The ultimate fire position,
(b) The most concealed line of approach,
(c) The formations to adopt at various stages of the advance. Two or more sections may be selected (according to the ground) to carry out the exercise; good and bad methods being shewn: the remainder will proceed to the objective and observe them.

Criticism.—The following points will be brought out:—

1. The same as in Exercise 1.
2. Leadership, handling and command of the Section.
3. Suitability of the formations adopted.

3rd Exercise.—The attack by two sections under battle conditions.

Object.—To practice Section Commanders in leading their Sections in an attack on a limited front, to use ground and cover if available, and how to create cover by means of fire.

Procedure.—The objective and limits of the ground that may be used are pointed out—these limits must not exceed the platoon frontage of $200^\times$.

Leaders will have to consider the following points:—
  (a) The amount of cover the ground affords.
  (b) The possibility of advancing without fire, and where it will be needed.
  (c) Suitable fire positions and how to approach them.
  (d) Formations to use and method of advance.

Points for Criticism:—
  (a) Ground and formations as in Exercise 2.
  (b) The combination of fire and movement, the timing of the mutual support.
  (c) The fire orders of the leaders, and fire discipline of the men.

MINOR TACTICAL EXERCISES.

The object of these exercises is to train fire unit leaders, Officers and N.C.Os., to work out minor tactical problems on the ground without troops.

The force whose action is considered in detail should usually be confined to the normal fire unit, *i.e.*, a section or platoon.

Notes and method of procedure.

  i. The Officer conducting the exercise should invariably go over the ground prior to carrying it out.

  ii. The exercise can conveniently take the form of a tactical walk in the country.

  iii. Students should be divided into syndicates of about 4 members each, one of whom will be appointed as leader to control his syndicate throughout the exercise.

  iv. Note books for writing down fire orders, instructions, &c., should be carried, also field glasses if possible.

  v. During the course of the exercise a series of definite situations will be given out and a definite solution asked for in each case: this will usually take the form of definite fire orders (properly given) or concise instructions to imaginary leaders or to a formation.
   Vague indefinite solutions are of no instructional value and must never be permitted, *e.g.*, in a solution involving the action of a section every man in the section (1 N.C.O. and 6 men) must be accounted for; in the case of a platoon the action and location of the two L.G. and two rifle sections and of Platoon Headquarters must be exactly indicated.

  vi. When a situation has been given out, the conducting officer, after a sufficient pause to enable all members of syndicates to discuss and consider the solution, will indicate a number (1, 2, 3 or 4) to act as spokesman in each syndicate. The spokesman in turn will detail the soluton arrived at: criticisms and if necessary, discussion will follow. This method will ensure all members of the party receiving practice in giving orders and instructions.

The following brief examples indicate suitable items for inclusion in a tactical walk or during hours devoted to minor tactical problems :—

Problem.	Notes.
1. Fire orders for a section or platoon. (Use of Rifle and L.G.)	A situation requiring some simple fire order, concentrated—distributed — anticipatory — hasty, should all be practised, and be given properly.
2. Sudden situations. (Use of Infantry formations.)	Platoon moving down a road, or in fours, comes under artillery or machine gun fire—orders to be issued as to what formation to adopt to resist fire and what line of country to take in order to make full use of the ground.
3. Occupation of a fire position.	Position to be occupied is indicated by conducting officer. Orders are to be given out for formations to be adopted in approaching fire position and line of advance. Exact location of sections on reaching fire position will be shown by students.
4. Reconnaissance before attack ; occupation of successive fire positions.	Objective pointed out and limits of frontage given by conducting officer. Ground is reconnoitred by syndicates by means of field glasses, and spokesmen describe successive fire positions to be occupied. Syndicates then move from position to position, which are examined, and a fire problem set at each.
5. Occupation of a fire position in defence. Selection of position for a picquet.	Conducting officer points out roughly position of picquet for one platoon by day or night, and indicates position of picquets on flanks. Syndicates select and detail exact position for sentries, and sections with a view to defence. Range orders drawn up. Co-operation and mutual assistance by fire. Location of obstacles, if necessary, described. Location and description of any necessary improvement in the picquet position ; trenches, wire, &c.

As progress made, students should be encouraged to " think in fire orders," and in the use of ground and suitable formations.

www.ingramcontent.com/pod-product-compliance
Lightning Source LLC
Chambersburg PA
CBHW031429040426
42444CB00006B/756